The Voice of Th

The Voice of This Calling

Eric James

morehouse

Morehouse
4775 Linglestown Road
Harrisburg
PA 17112

Continuum
The Tower Building
11 York Road
London, SE1 7NX

Morehouse is an imprint of Continuum Books

www.continuumbooks.com

© Eric James 2005

Little Gidding by T. S. Eliot reproduced with permission of Faber and Faber

First published 2005

British Library Cataloguing-in-Publication Data
A catalogue record for this book is available from The British Library.

ISBN 0-8192-8120-4

Typeset by BookEns Ltd, Royston, Herts.
Printed and bound in Great Britain by Cromwell Press, Trowbridge, Wilts

Contents

Preface   vii

1 *Japes*: St Paul's Church, Covent Garden, 4 March 2001   1
2 The things I see: Horsham Parish Church, St Mary the   8
   Virgin, 11 March 2001
3 The annual service of the Order of St John of Jerusalem: 15
   St Paul's Cathedral, 23 June 2001
4 Discovering our priesthood: St Mary's, Hendon,   19
   3 July 2001
5 Faith and music: St Margaret's, King's Lynn, 29 July 2001   24
6 Remembrance Day: Westminster Abbey, 11 November 2001   30
7 Christian hope: The Chapel Royal, St James's Palace,   36
   30 December 2001
8 The Soper sermon: Soper, Simeon and the spirituality of   40
   ageing: The West London Methodist Mission, Hinde
   Street, 27 January 2002
9 A lamb to the slaughter: St Mary Abbots', Kensington,   48
   17 February 2002
10 All you need is love: St Saviour's, Pimlico, 9 June 2002   54
11 'Who do *you* say that I am?': Matthew 16: 15, St Mary's
   Lewisham, 30 June 2002   58
12 St Mary Magdalene Patronal Festival: St Mary   63
   Magdalene, Richmond, 21 July 2002
13 The fiftieth anniversary of my ordination to the priest-   68
   hood: St Stephen's Rochester Row, 29 September 2002

Contents

14 Remembrance Day: St Mary's Primrose Hill,   76
    10 November 2002

15 The installation of Anthony Hawley as Canon   82
    Residentiary of Liverpool: Liverpool Cathedral,
    30 November 2002

16 Gallipoli Memorial Service: Holy Trinity, Eltham,   91
    13 April 2003

17 The funeral of the Revd Frank Seymour ('Bill') Skelton: 100
    Southwark Cathedral, 5 June 2003

18 'What must I do to win eternal life?': Mark 10: 17–31,   108
    St Margaret's, Lee, 12 October 2003

19 Memorial service for Andrew Hake: St Margaret's   112
    Church, Oxford, 18 October 2003

20 The funeral service of Canon Paul Jobson: St Saviour's   119
    Pimlico, 7 November 2003

21 How to look: The Chapel Royal, St James's Palace,   127
    4 January 2004

22 'The trumpet shall sound . . . and we shall be changed':   132
    1 Cor. 15: 52, BBC Radio 4 Sunday Worship,
    St Martin-in-the-Fields, 8 February 2004

23 Memorial service for Daniel George Goyder: St Mary-   136
    le-Tower, Ipswich, 22 March 2004

24 175th King's College Anniversary Alumni Weekend: 142
    Sung Evensong, the Chapel of King's College London,
    11 June 2004

25 The fiftieth anniversary of the ordination of the   147
    Revd John Baker: St Luke's, Battersea, 4 July 2004

Preface

Now I am in my eightieth year, my memories of earlier years are often vivid.

In 1942 – when I was 17 – ten years before my ordination – I went into Alfred Wilson's bookshop in the City and bought the latest T. S. Eliot poem, the fourth of his *Four Quartets* – *Little Gidding* – published as a separate booklet: a paperback, price one shilling. (I had bought from the same bookshop the first three of the *Quartets*, as they were published in 1940 and 1941.)

Little Gidding has some unforgettable lines and images: 'What we call the beginning is often the end . . .'. One line, over the years, has seemed to increase its power: 'With the drawing of this Love and the Voice of this Calling . . .'.

I had no doubt that I wanted to call what may well be my last book, *The Voice of This Calling* for it has seemed to say, and sum up, so much about the vocation of the preacher.

Inevitably, this final volume of my sermons includes several preached at the funerals and memorial services of my friends. I do not apologize for including them. No period of my ministry has been more privileged – or more painful and demanding – than this last. 'Words fail.' One can only trust and obey 'the Voice of this Calling'.

I am thankful for all who have given me their support and friendship from before my ordination until now – this fifty-third year since my ordination.

My thanks go to Jane Spurr, who has again kindly typed the manuscript of this volume, and also to Robin Baird-Smith, my publisher.

Eric James
25 July 2004

1 *Japes*: St Paul's Church, Covent Garden, 4 March 2001

I want first to thank my good friend, Mark Oakley, your *relatively* new vicar, for inviting me to preach this morning, and to preach on a play of my choice. And I want to thank Michael Redington, my friend of more than 40 years, for putting me on to *Japes*, and, indeed for giving me a couple of tickets for the first night.

I had no idea what I was in for; but I took with me another Michael – another friend, who's now a Harley Street psychiatrist. Michael Perring is one of four brothers, and comes in the middle of three; but has lived with the guilt of the death-at-birth of the fourth – his twin.

Playwrights write autobiographically – some more than others, And playgoers watch and listen autobiographically. So Michael seemed the right sort of person to take with me to *Japes*. But perhaps I'd better confess that I am myself the younger of two brothers. My brother is four years older than I. He, too, is a priest and preacher. But two brothers in the same profession could hardly be more different.

And while I'm confessing, perhaps I should add, that I well remember, when I was a child, standing on a chair, next to the open back door of our house – open on to the garden. It was summer time. I was behind the door; and I had in my hand my brother's cricket bat. I was hoping that he would come in through that door, when I would be able to bring down the cricket bat onto his skull! Mercifully, he decided to come in through the sitting room door, thus approaching me from behind, and saying: 'What are you doing there with my cricket bat?'

1

But enough said. I simply wanted to make it clear that if anyone's autobiography equipped them to appreciate *Japes*, I could confidently claim to be he.

There's just one thing more I want to say before we get on to the play. There's a problem about preaching on a current play – though it's the problem every critic faces: how to talk about a play at length – and in depth – without revealing the heart of the matter. In a 'Who dunnit?', that means, of course, avoiding Who diddit? But what to avoid in a more complex and profound play is, of course, more complex and profound.

Lastly – lastly, by way of introduction! – the readings this morning – Cain and Abel and the Prodigal Son – were not accidents. They were chosen to remind you – and me – that we're not here simply to hear another piece of theatre criticism. My task is, of course, different: to preach the Gospel; but to do so by relating it to *Japes*: to the realities of *Japes*.

The better the play, the more likely it is to have something profound to say about the meaning of being truly human. And by that arbitrament, *Japes*, to me, is a very considerable play.

For those who've not seen it – not yet seen it – may I say, briefly, that it's a tale of two brothers. Jason, known as 'Japes', who's been crippled in a diving-board accident, which Michael – 'Michey' – reproaches himself for not preventing. The two brothers share the flat they've inherited. There they live in affectionate competitive hostility. They share Anita – or 'Neets'. Michey is her official lover – to to speak – and a struggling novelist. Neets actually finds Japes more exciting as a lover than Michey. But Japes goes off and teaches English in South America. So Michey is more 'reliable' – it can be said – especially as Japes, when he returns, is a wreck: a victim of drink and drugs, and what drink and drugs provoke.

The play covers 27 years. So Michey and Neets, in due course, are married. But Japes and Neets are soon together again. And no one quite knows which of the two brothers is the father of Neets' daughter, Wendy. Grown-up Wendy comes into her own in the last scene.

My friend Michael and I were both gripped by the first act. It's one of those plays when the interval – when you're supposed to go out, and down drinks, and chat – was almost a blasphemy. When the curtain comes down on that act, you want simply to be silent – or, rather, you want to rush on to the stage, and put your arms round the wounded brother, on whom the curtain has descended. The play evokes from within you the father whom Rembrandt unforgettably painted in *The Return of the Prodigal*. And any play which can evoke such a father within one – such a comforter; such a desire to lift the burden of transgression; to assuage the pain; to bless, and heal, and forgive – any play that can create such a desire in an audience is a great play. And my friend, Michael, and I both found ourselves with such emotions.

And I'll not tell you which of the sons, at the end of that first act, drew such emotions from us. I have to say: it is one of the greatest moments in the theatre I've ever experienced.

Great theatrical moments are, of course, not simply the product of the playwright, or of the actors, or of the director. They take the whole team. *Japes* is a play of great acting: by Toby Stephens as 'Japes'; by Jasper Britton as 'Michey'; by Clare Swinburne as 'Neets', and, later, as Wendy. It's marvellously written by Simon Gray, and superbly directed by Peter Hall.

The second Act is, to my mind, less convincing than the first – not least because the first Act has been so powerful. What happens to Michey, who becomes a successful novelist, as the literary world understands success, is convincing. So, too, is what happens to Japes. But what happens to the adult Wendy – after her mother's death – is not wholly convincing. (I must not say more.)

Japes is a play that depends above all on its realism.

Its pain is real.

Its sexual enjoyment is real.

Its competitiveness between brothers and its brotherly affection are real.

Its jealousy and envy are real.

Its humour is real – not least, about the Garrick!

Its embarrassments are real.

The language of the play is real – God knows! – it's 'in your face' – 'all disguises off' – though I believe it will soon be seen to be inadequate, indeed, inaccurate, to think that 'in your face' descriptions of sexual behaviour do much more than trivialize the great mystery of human sexuality: the great mystery of intimacy.

But to continue: real people – real brothers – do fall in love with the same people. The guilt and self-disgust in *Japes* are real. Japes' own pomposity, decline and fall are real – so, too, is Michey's growing up. The teenage Wendy's friendship with her uncle is real. And with parents like Wendy's, it's real enough to 'go berserk'. (As I've said: I must not say more.) As the critic, Georgina Brown, wrote: '*Japes* is heart-rendingly real.'

And it's spiced with wonderful lines from Wordsworth, Eliot, and Empson – and from Simon Gray himself. He makes Michey speak of 'the sheer drudgery of being me'.

But there's one passage in Act two: Scene three when Japes and Michey are talking together, when I believe the play could have at least suggested 'possibilities' which may have given it an even greater greatness.

The successful Michey is to appear on TV, talking about the 'recurrent themes of his fictions – loss and betrayal'. He talks of 'the whiff of redemption in my prose, my latest prose' which some have recognized. 'I don't actually think it's redemption,' he says: 'More an acceptance, an informed acceptance of the nature of things.' In other words: it's another example of realism – 'an informed acceptance of the nature of things'.

There is in *Japes* a decline into pomposity; obsession with alcohol and drugs – and sex; and betrayal; and some sort of suicide. And there's at one point, from one character, an animal howl of grief that sounds like Christ's cry on Calvary: 'My God, my God, why hast thou forsaken me?'

But Simon Gray makes no attempt whatever to articulate in any of his characters a cry for redemption. If redemption exists, none of the characters in *Japes* seems to know anything about it – though they do know what I will call 'negative incapability'.

Truly great theatre always, surely, has 'the whiff of redemption' – and more than the whiff – about it. It's never just about going to hell, however real that journey to hell and experience of it may be. It needs to take us at least to the doors of the mystery of redemption.

It's in the very last scene of the last act of *Lear* – after all that he has endured – that he invites Cordelia with him to:

> take upon's the mystery of things,
> As if we were God's spies.

Many of us who are here this morning, are, I imagine, only here because we believe that redemption is as real as any of the events recorded in *Japes*. Indeed, *Japes* may be thought of by at least some of us as a 'cautionary tale' – where we might all be, but for Redemption.

It was not only the Father-of-the-Prodigal in me who wanted to leap on to the stage at the end of the first Act; it was someone who over the years has learnt the meaning of redemption in his deep heart's core, and who longed to share what he had learnt.

The world of *Japes* seemed never to have heard of the world of Bach's *St Matthew Passion* or to have looked on that painting to which I've already referred – Rembrandt's *The Return of the Prodigal Son* – that pathetic, bedraggled, emaciated young man, so embraced on his return that the return itself became a resurrection: from Death to Life. I found myself wondering, with a smile, whether Japes had thought of popping into the National Gallery, to that remarkable exhibition *Seeing Salvation*.

I do not want this morning to end what I have to say with a kind of theology of redemption. The response to Simon Gray's marvellous text must not be 'systematic theology'. I think this morning it must be a poem. How I should like to have read some R. S. Thomas to Michey, and Japes, and Neeta and Wendy. Maybe – as a grateful response to *Japes* – I'll read to you George Herbert's poem:

5

The Flower:

How fresh, O Lord, how sweet and clean
Are thy returns! Ev'n as the flowers in spring,
　　To which, besides their own demean,
The late-past frosts tributes of pleasure bring.
　　　　Grief melts away
　　　　Like snow in May,
　　As if there were no such cold thing.

　　Who would have thought my shrivel'd heart
Could have recover'd greennesse? It was gone
　　Quite under ground, as flowers depart
To see their mother-root when they have blown;
　　　　Where they together
　　　　All the hard weather,
　　Dead to the world, keep house unknown.

　　These are thy wonders, Lord of power,
Killing and quickning, bringing down to hell
　　And up to heaven in an houre;
Making a chiming of a passing-bell.
　　　　We say amisse,
　　　　This or that is;
　　Thy word is all, if we could spell.

　　O that I once past changing were,
Fast in thy Paradise, where no flower can wither!
　　Many a spring I shoot up fair,
Off'ring at heav'n, growing and groning thither,
　　　　Nor doth my flower
　　　　Want a spring-showre,
　　My sinnes and I joining together.

　　But while I grow in a straight line,
Still upwards bent, as if heav'n were mine own,

Thy anger comes, and I decline.
What frost to that? What pole is not the zone
    Where all things burn,
    When thou dost turn,
    And the least frown of thine is shown?

And now in age I bud again,
After so many deaths I live and write;
    I once more smell the dew and rain,
And relish versing, O my only light,
    It cannot be
    That I am he
On whom thy tempests fell all night.

These are thy wonders, Lord of love,
To make us see we are but flowers that glide.
    Which when we once can finde and prove,
Thou hast a garden for us where to bide.
    Who would be more
    Swelling through store,
Forfeit their Paradise by their pride.

2 The things I see: Horsham Parish Church, St Mary the Virgin, 11 March 2001

I was delighted to receive your vicar's kind invitation to me to preach to you today on the theme which all your Sunday preachers this Lent have been given: 'The things I see'.

Well, what do I see?

First of all, unless my eyes deceive me, I think I see a congregation, gathered in their parish church: this historic and beautiful church. But, although that may sound like a 'glimpse of the obvious', you'll understand if I say I literally don't know what I'm talking about. I don't know *you*.

At first sight, I see a congregation gathered in their parish church; but I suspect that there are many and various reasons why you are here this morning – in your parish church. I would, for instance, be interested to know how many of you are, in fact, parishioners – legal parishioners of St Mary's, Horsham. Indeed, it would be fascinating to find out just why each one of you has 'congregated' here this morning – so that I see you. And it would be no less fascinating to find out what that word 'parish' means to each one of you.

You see, at one time most people lived, and worked, and spent their leisure within the parish; but now, people work in one parish, live in another, and in their leisure time they are under the influence of another 'world', so to speak – the TV, and so on. The parish church at one time related to all the worlds that people inhabited; but now . . . Well, what worlds of yours does the parish church of Horsham relate to?

Put it another way: I should like to know whether the congregation I see brings all your life with you into Horsham Parish Church today. How does the parish church relate to the whole of you? Or does the split in the life of modern man, and woman, radically alter what religion now affects?

Your former bishop, Simon Phipps – who, alas, died so recently – wrote a book called *God on Monday.* What effect will Horsham Parish Church have on its congregation at, say, eleven o'clock this Monday morning? That's my point. Now I see you. Then I won't!

Let me repeat my question. 'The things I see' this morning? – first: a congregation gathered in the parish church. But why? Some of you may say: 'I love the way they do things here – the way we worship. And the sermons are always interesting (except when there's a visiting preacher!). And the building means a lot to me.'

Some people may say: 'I've been a "St Mary's person" for years.' Others may say: 'Well, I don't get here very regularly; but I'm glad Horsham Parish Church is here, whether I'm here or not.'

What I'm underlining is that what I see, as a complete stranger – a congregation – is made up of people with varying experiences; with private griefs, joys, sins, temperaments, psyches, reasons for thanksgiving; but what I see from this pulpit today is, literally, the 'top surface'.

Some husbands will be here 'cos the wife's here. Some wives will be here 'cos the husband's here – or 'cos the children are here.

I see a congregation. But 'congregation' is an odd word. I'm saying the 'why' beneath the surface of the fact of your congregating is all-important.

I travel about the C of E a good deal, and meet many people who say: 'I don't go to my *parish* church 'cos they have women priests there.' Or 'I used to go to the parish church; but I can't stand the new vicar.' The parish church is always 'there'; but each church member has to choose to congregate – or not! There are reasons why people are attracted to, and why they're put off the parish church, which are significant.

Forty years ago, when I was vicar of the inner-city parish church of St George's Camberwell, I went one Sunday evening in Lent to preach at Sanderstead. The vicar kindly met me at the station, and said: 'Eric, I'm so glad you've come. I couldn't bear the thought of your having such a small congregation every week. We get a large congregation.' And he added: 'It all seems to work here.' I immediately threw away my sermon, and preached on: 'It all seems to work here.' I asked: 'Is it the Cross that works here? Why is it that middle-class Sanderstead gets more in its congregation than inner-city Camberwell? Irrespective of who's the vicar.' And so on.

In Kennington, where I live now – in the Parish Church of St Anselm's, Kennington – the congregation this morning will be mostly black. That's *what I see* in Kennington.

If your background was Irish, you'd probably not be here, you'd be in Horsham's RC Church. A congregation is affected by class, and race, and, indeed, the age structure of the surrounding population, and what we now call their 'mobility'.

When I've previously come to Horsham – in the past 50 years – Horsham was a very different place. I remember Ronnie Goodchild here in the 1950s – before they replanned the centre of Horsham. How has the congregation coped with change, I wonder? Or have most of you moved into Horsham since most of the change?

When I've come to Horsham, most often I've come to Christ's Hospital to preach. When you look up Horsham in the *Oxford Literary Guide to the British Isles*, it says under 'Horsham': 'See Christ's Hospital'! What effect has Christ's Hospital had on Horsham Parish Church over the last hundred years of its history? Is Christ's Hospital a separate world? I suspect it is.

Horsham Parish Church isn't a separate world: it belongs to a diocese. Do you as a congregation feel yourself to be part of Chichester Diocese? Your suffragan bishop, Lindsay Urwin, came from Australia, and was a curate, when I first met him, in the Walworth Road, not far from where I live now. He was ordained in 1980 and served in Inner South London for eight years. Lindsay connects you not only to Chichester Diocese but to the inner city.

In Horsham Parish Church this morning 'What do I see?' I see a congregation gathered for worship. But I wonder what you think worship is. That's worth asking every one of you. What does worship mean to you? Has your capacity for worship grown over the years? I see a congregation of worshippers – but each one different.

I'd love to hear your definition of worship. Mine is: 'Worship is the response of all that I am to all that I know God to be.' And because I am different from you, and you from me, although we are involved in 'common worship', it will be different for each one of us. We're all at different stages in worship. Not least because, frankly, we don't all take worship all that seriously – perhaps not as seriously as we take golf, or embroidery, or our investments! Prayer and worship need to be worked at.

I see a congregation of worshippers. And I've just seen a congregation listening to the reading of Scripture – listening, for instance, to today's Gospel. And I said to myself: 'I wonder what each member of the congregation is making of the Gospel as it's read?'

Do you remember – in the Gospel – the four words: 'Go tell that fox'? What did they mean to you? To 'fox' is, of course, to cheat. It's to be crafty. 'A dog, a weasel and a fox sleep with one eye open' runs the saying. 'Go tell that fox' – (don't worry; I'm not going to go on about fox hunting!).

In the Gospel, the situation is clear. The Pharisees, who come to warn Jesus of Herod's intention, posed as friends. They might have guessed Jesus would be suspicious of their solicitude for his safety: that He would recognize they were in collusion with Herod – 'that fox'. If ever they thought – or we thought – of Jesus simply as Charles Wesley's hymn describes him: as 'Gentle Jesus, meek and mild', these four words – 'Go tell that fox' – tell us to think again.

I myself have found this text useful on more than one occasion, when I needed to address those in power – in church as well as state. Bishops, politicians, local government officers, employers, lawyers, trades union officials: we can all be foxes at times.

Sometimes it's easy to 'tell that fox', if you're, say, a Churchill, and you have a Hitler in mind. But it's much more difficult if you're, say,

Dietrich Bonhoeffer, who died in a Nazi concentration camp in 1945.

Let me tell you my favourite story of Bonhoeffer. In 1933, he came over here, to South London – to be Minister of the German Church here – in Forest Hill. In 1935 he went back to be head of a theological college. Of his 150 students, 80 were eventually killed in action during the Second World War.

In 1940, he took one of his students – Eberhard Bethge – who eventually became his biographer – to Memel, in East Prussia. They were sitting in the garden of a café, outside the town, when the news came over the radio, with a fanfare of trumpets, that Paris had fallen. Immediately the little garden was in a joyful uproar. Men and women jumped to their feet, breaking into the National Anthem and the Horst Wessel song. They raised their arms in the Nazi salute. Bethge, the student, remained rooted to his seat; but he was surprised to see Bonhoeffer lustily joining in the singing and saluting. Bonhoeffer whispered to Bethge, 'Put up your arm. Are you crazy? This thing isn't worth dying for,' he said, pointing to his arm. 'You've got to know when to die' – when your hour has come. Five years later, as I've said, Bonhoeffer died, in a concentration camp. But in 1940 he had to be crafty – to be a fox.

In his last three years – in prison – he worked on his great unfinished book, simply called *Ethics*. Let me read you three short sentences from it:

> In a world where success is the measure and justification of all things, the figure of Him who was sentenced and crucified remains a stranger, and is at best the object of pity. The world will allow itself to be subdued only by success.
>
> The figure of the Crucified invalidates all thought which takes success for its standard.

'Go tell that fox.' Sometimes you have to stand up to foxes in the name and in the power of Christ. Sometimes you have to *be* a fox in the name and in the power of Christ.

Of course, it won't do to think that those four words are all that Jesus had to say by way of example. Yet it's important that we hear those four words: hear them in the congregation, in the parish church; and we must think what they have to say to us in the different departments of our life. That's the purpose of what I saw each one of you doing: listening to the Gospel.

What do I see?

I have said in several ways that I see a congregation gathered in Horsham Parish Church.

As, once, a parish priest myself – many long years ago! – I have to say, with the voice of experience, that there is a negative side to gathering in parish churches. We are in Horsham, not Gatwick, not Brighton. Often, historic churches, as was mine in Camberwell, can be rocks in an ocean of change, to which people cling for dear life. They can be 'shelters from the stormy blast'. They can be refuges from refugees. They can exclude and keep out. But at Horsham Parish you won't need to be given that warning.

I've already mentioned this morning the name of your erstwhile Bishop of Horsham, Simon Phipps. The simple fact is that no one affected my life more than Simon. Thirty years ago he got me to be Chaplain of Trinity College, Cambridge, with him – and we remained friends for life.

Just over a month ago, on a Saturday, he phoned me and asked me to come to his eightieth birthday party, in July. I was overjoyed and said 'Yes!' The Tuesday after that phone call, he died. I came to his funeral near here, at Shipley, on Monday the twelfth of last month.

What do I see as I look at you today? I see a congregation journeying through life: ageing like Simon Phipps – and me: journeying towards death. I preach to you 'as a dying man to dying men and women'.

As Charles Wesley wrote:

> One family, we dwell in him,
>   One Church, above, beneath;

Though now divided by the stream,
The narrow stream of death.

One army of the living God,
To his command we bow;
Part of his host have crossed the flood,
And part are crossing now.

E'en now to their eternal home
There pass some spirits blest
While others to the margin come
Waiting their call to rest.

Jesu, be thou our constant Guide,
Then when the word is given,
Bid Jordan's narrow stream divide,
And bring us safe to heaven.

That's 'The things I see' from your pulpit this morning.

3 The Annual Service of the Order of St John of Jerusalem: St Paul's Cathedral, 23 June 2001

Cufflinks Howard: I'd be surprised if more than a handful of you knew him. He's been dead for many years now. I remember him when I was a child. And I shall never forget him.

'Remind me,' I said to my sister – who's well over 80 now – 'Remind me why he was called *Cufflinks* Howard?'

'Well,' she said, 'In November 1928, King George V was taken very ill with pleurisy and pneumonia. After his illness, by February 1929, he was well enough to convalesce, and was taken to Bognor. It has to be said, he didn't greatly enjoy Bognor. Rumour has it that he used a very rude word about it! But, ever after, Bognor was allowed to call itself Bognor *Regis* – as it does to this day.'

'Yes. Yes,' I said to my sister. 'But what about *Cufflinks* Howard? Why *Cufflinks* Howard?'

'Oh. Don't you remember?' she said. 'Captain Howard – Captain Eric Howard – lived round the corner from us. He was in the St John Ambulance Brigade, and was one of the stretcher-bearers who carried King George V when he went by ambulance to Bognor. And the king rewarded him – and all the stretcher-bearers – with a marvellous pair of cufflinks for each of them, which he gave them personally at Buckingham Palace. And, ever after, Eric Howard was known locally as *Cufflinks* Howard.'

'Ah, yes,' I said, 'And I always remember him looking very smart in

15

his St John Ambulance uniform.' I've remembered him for over 70 years.

Examples are powerful – for good *and* evil. *Cufflinks Howard* was a memorable example for good. And his wife and his daughter were both in St John Ambulance with him, for years.

Examples are, of course, of many sorts.

Until recently, I was the Director of a charity called Christian Action. And I've been fascinated for years by the subject of giving to charity. But I don't mean only the giving of money.

Let me give you another 'brief life': another example. Richard Titmuss was born in Luton. His father was an unsuccessful farmer, who died when Richard was 19, leaving him to support the family. He went out to work – as an office boy, at Standard Telephones. Then, for 16 years, he worked in an insurance office. He never sat an examination; but he worked likes blazes in public libraries.

He had his first book – *Poverty and Population* – published in 1938. It won acclaim from Harold Macmillan, and the Rowntrees and the Cadburys.

Richard had a passion for social justice and a strong sense of public duty. I mention him today not least because he was a member of the firewatchers' squad, here at St Paul's, who, in 1940, saved this great cathedral from destruction. That's just one example of Richard's public spirit.

His greatest book was about blood doning. He called it *The Gift Relationship*. Richard wasn't a very religious person; but he said that nothing brought him nearer to belief in God than his study of blood doning. 'What is it?' he kept asking himself, 'that gives people such a deep-seated desire to help others – people they've never met – the desire to help them anonymously, and for no financial reward?'

Those whom he questioned came up with different answers. 'I do it to help the hospitals' some said. 'It's a way of saying "thank you" for my own good health', said others. And others: 'You never know: you might be saving someone's life'; and others: 'Well, it might be you next time.'

I should emphasize that Richard found this 'altruism' – as it's called – this concern to help others – in people of different races, of different religions, and of none.

Titmuss' study included a comparison of different ways of procuring blood in different societies. They varied from complete reliance on voluntary donors to accepting the free play of market forces – procuring the blood at the price it could command on the open market. It was from this comparison of his that Titmuss concluded that the commercialization of blood donor relationships suppressed the expression of this capacity we have to help others. And he became a passionate enthusiast for voluntarily helping others.

I find it important simply to reflect on the fact that we all have this remarkable capacity. I'd want to suggest that any human being who does not take it seriously is neglecting a very important part of themselves. And I'd go further, and say that if we take time and care about this deep-seated desire and capacity – which is part of us all by our very creation – we may discover part of ourselves we hardly knew existed. And I suppose this capacity for helping others is revealed in the work of the Order of St John, and the Red Cross, as much as in any other organization you can name.

Richard Titmuss – by the way – became Professor Richard Titmuss and a Commander of the British Empire – which has its Chapel here in the crypt of this cathedral.

One day, in 1973, I chanced to look out from the top of a bus that had just crossed Lambeth Bridge from south to north, to see Richard standing on the pavement, looking very frail. I jumped off the bus and greeted him. 'Eric', he said, 'get me a taxi, please. I've just discharged myself from the Westminster Hospital with inoperable cancer.' Richard died, alas, only a few weeks later. I think of him as a marvellous human example.

St John of Jerusalem. He, too, was an example.

When I knew I was to have the honour of preaching to you today, I asked a friend which St John St John of Jerusalem was. 'Oh,' he said, 'There's only one St John.' 'No,' I said. 'There's St John the Apostle.

There's St John the Divine – who wrote the last book of the Bible. There's St John the Baptist. There's a dozen St Johns.'

Your St John – of Jerusalem – I discovered – much to my surprise – was someone whom most people know as John the Baptist. The Knights Hospitallers had their headquarters, at the end of the eleventh century, at a hospital in Jerusalem under the patronage of St John the Baptist. He had clearly been an example to them.

In a sentence: What kind of example had John the Baptist been?

A rather unusual kind, I think.

He pointed to Jesus as his example. He pointed away from himself. He was devoid of pomposity. Perhaps his most famous saying is: 'I'm not worthy to unloose the latchet of the shoes of Jesus.' John the Baptist was an example – a rare example – of humility: and of discernment and judgement. 'Jesus,' he said, 'is the man really to be your example.'

As I said at the beginning: 'Examples are powerful and are of all sorts: good and evil.'

And you have to choose. Nowadays, we call examples 'role models' and 'icons'. I wonder whom you choose for your example. And, just as important, I wonder what kind of an example you set to others.

Cufflinks Howard; Richard Titmuss; John the Baptist; Jesus.

To be human is to have the capacity to set an example – for good or ill.

The Order of St John has set a superb example over the centuries – not least in support of the marvellous St John of Jerusalem Eye Hospital.

Let us today give thanks for all who, by the grace of God, have been our example.

Let us today rededicate ourselves to be, by the grace of God, an example to others.

And let us thank God particularly for the example of the St John who said of Jesus, 'I'm not worthy to untie his shoelaces.'

4 Discovering our priesthood: St Mary's, Hendon, 3 July 2001

I count it a very great privilege to be asked by my young friend, my great friend, Stuart Owen, to preach on this first occasion that he presides at the Holy Communion.

It cannot but take me back to my own ordination as a priest – 50 years ago next year. And it cannot but remind me what changes there have been – in the Church and the world – in those 50 years. And it cannot but take all of us here back two thousand years, to 'the same night that he was betrayed' when 'Jesus took bread, and when he had given thanks, he broke it and gave it to his disciples, saying, "Take, eat; this is my body."' And it cannot but make each one of us lift up our hearts and minds to Him who is the Author and Finisher of our life, our faith, and our ministry, in Christ.

There are several people whom I would love to have been present this evening – and, indeed, to have come to know you, Stuart.

Eric Abbott, Dean of King's College, London, and, later, Dean of Westminster, who, 50 years ago – as Stuart will be tired of hearing – taught me much of whatever I know about priesthood. He died in 1983.

Eric Abbott also had a friend-and-mentor, Alexander Nairne, a scholar and theologian, who died in 1936, having been Professor of Hebrew and Old Testament at King's College, London, and then Professor of Divinity at Cambridge. Perhaps his greatest book was called *The Epistle of Priesthood*. It is a commentary on the Epistle to the

Hebrews. And at the heart of that book there is a memorable definition of a priest, as 'One who stands on the manward side of God and the Godward side of man.'

Such a phrase these days has somehow to be purged of what we call its 'non-inclusive language' – offensive to some. But for 50 years that phrase, I have to say, has stood me in good stead as perhaps the profoundest definition of priesthood I know: 'One who stands on the human side of God and the Godward side of humanity.'

But what does that mean? What should it mean? What can it mean? What must it mean to you, Stuart, as you face a very different world from the world I faced 50 years ago, but yet a world which is also remarkably the same? 'The human side of God, and the Godward side of humanity'?

Perhaps this is the point at which I should say that although, as I've said, I felt greatly privileged to be asked to preach at what is sometimes called a 'first Mass', I always wince a little, if and when that phrase is used, because, after he's ordained, the primary job of a priest is not to say: 'Now I'm a priest!' It's to turn to each member of the congregation, and to all his friends and family, and to say, silently: 'It's my job to remind you of your priesthood. It's my job to help you in any way I can to discover your priesthood – whatever your job in life: in the home; or at work; or even out of work. Whatever you do in the church or the world: everyone's a priest.'

Sometimes when we go to a concert, we hear an instrument of the orchestra announce a theme; but by the end of the work, whatever it is, all the instruments of the orchestra have taken up that theme, and it becomes – let's say – a symphony.

On Sunday, Stuart was ordained priest, and was commissioned to announce the theme of priesthood. But it isn't his theme. That theme was announced most clearly in the life and triumphant suffering of Jesus. And Stuart's here now to help each one of us take up that theme on our instruments: some of us more percussion than strings! Some of us brass! Some of us woodwind! Some of us more vocalists than instrumentalists!

But how do we keep that theme of the priesthood clear? How do we announce it to our modern secular world with the clarity that's required?

The first reading this evening came from a favourite Old Testament passage of mine: from the Book of the Prophet Habbakuk. It began: 'I will climb my watchtower' – which reminded me of another person I would have much liked you, Stuart, and, indeed, everyone, to have met: Canon Max Warren, who died in 1977. He was a Canon of Westminster, with Eric Abbott, after he'd been head of the Church Missionary Society for 20 years. He was a pioneer of inter-faith dialogue, so had a great concern for relating the Christian faith to other religions.

I only got one prize when I was at university, at King's College, London, but I'm very proud of it; because it's by Max Warren, and called *The Truth of Vision: A Study in the Nature of Christian Hope*. And I've treasured it for over 50 years. And this is how it begins:

> Habbakuk, like the other prophets of Israel, grappled with the perplexities and fears of his age. As he sought to find a meaning in contemporary events, God spoke to him, and revealed Himself as the Lord of all history. From this revelation springs the Biblical understanding of Hope.
>
> The application of this truth to our own age demands an attempt to achieve a sympathetic understanding of the events of our time, and to see the Church set in the midst of those events to serve the purposes of God. This is no easy task. It is costly in sympathy and patience.

But that's why Habbakuk climbed his watchtower. And every priest – and every Christian, in their priesthood – has to do just that. We have to be faithful and disciplined in climbing our watchtower.

That reading from Habbakuk comes as a reading for St Thomas's Day, whom we all know as 'Doubting' Thomas. But I suspect we ought to think of him more as 'Questioning' Thomas. And it was T. S. Eliot who wrote in a poem:

O my Soul, be prepared for the coming of the Stranger
Be prepared for him who knows how to ask questions.

Stuart, I suspect, from what I know of you, you will always know how to ask questions; and I think, as part of your priesthood, and as part of your helping others to discover their priesthood, you will rightly spend a good deal of time helping others to ask questions.

You may have noticed that I have already mentioned this evening three people who have all been long since dead, but whom, Stuart, I would have wanted to join in your 'first Mass'. And I want to add one more: Robert Runcie, whom, just over a year ago, you will well remember, you pushed around the grounds of Cuddesdon Theological College in a wheelchair, only weeks before he died. He wrote to me, as you know, saying how much he had enjoyed meeting you that day and being 'pushed around' by you!

Besides passing on to you today that phrase of Alexander Nairne about priesthood – 'The human side of God and the Godward side of humanity' – I want to pass on to you this particular evening a not dissimilar phrase of Robert Runcie's about the meaning of priesthood. I give it to you, so to speak, on his behalf. 'A priest,' he said, 'has to be with God for other people and with other people for the sake of God.'

I've mentioned Eric Abbott and Alexander Nairne, and Max Warren, and Robert Runcie, because the older I get, the more at the Eucharist that phrase 'Therefore with angels and archangels and with all the company of heaven' means to me.

We who are gathered here this evening are only a fragment of the Church. And our earthly life is *very brief – so very brief.*

We know very little about the world beyond this. As St Paul said: 'Now we know in part, then shall we know even as we are known.' But priesthood is bound to be very concerned with that 'undiscovered country' as well as with this.

And sometimes it's as though the ramparts of heaven were crowded with those we love but see no longer, who are cheering us on, and assisting us with their prayers. Tonight is such a night: when 'earth's crammed with heaven'.

Dear Stuart, May you be as great a blessing to many in your ministry as you have already been to me, as you help them to understand 'the human side of God and the Godward side of humanity' and as you are 'with God for other people and with other people for the sake of God'.

5 Faith and music: St Margaret's, King's Lynn, 29 July 2001

It's lovely to return to St Margaret's. Some of you even remember my spending a month in the vicarage in August 1980 as a sort of substitute vicar, when Geoffrey Lang, your then vicar, was on holiday. Now your vicar has done me the great honour of asking me to preach at the end of your Festival, and during the celebration of your 900th Anniversary. How should we gather those two events together?

Well, I've decided to preach this morning on 'Faith and music' and there are some aspects of that which may gather both subjects and the past as well as the present. So, first, let me say something about creation and music. A couple of months ago, I was taken to a concert in the Royal Festival Hall in London. It was a recital given by the great pianist Alfred Brendel. To celebrate his seventieth birthday, he was playing the *Diabelli Variations* by Beethoven: 33 variations on a waltz. The publisher, Diabelli, commissioned 50 composers to write one variation each on that waltz theme he'd provided. These composers included Schubert and the 11-year-old Liszt. Beethoven's contribution developed, as I say, into 33 variations, and is one of his most important piano works – not performed all that often.

When Alfred Brendel came on to the platform that evening, I was suddenly overcome by the thought that I was present at a wonderful act of creation. These variations would never have been played quite like they would be played that evening. And, at the end of that performance, I was sure that was true.

24

There was no interval. Brendel sat there for nearly an hour, bringing those 33 variations to life.

I was overwhelmed by the thought of this unique act of creation. It was an unforgettable experience. But it was not only Brendel's act of creation that overwhelmed me. He was revealing Beethoven's act of creation when he composed those variations. And it wasn't only that that overwhelmed me. Brendel and Beethoven both revealed the marvel of our human capacity for creation – and yet few things make me believe in God more than this human capacity to create. The last thing Beethoven or Brendel would want to write is: 'All my own work'.

And it's not only the capacity to create music that's marvellous. Dare I say it: I perpetually marvel even at the gift of creating a sermon! (You may, of course, disagree!) But every time I write a sermon, I need to realize that the gift is a gift of God. But that's true whether it's words, or music, or gardening, or creating a steak and kidney pudding!

And I simply want to affirm, or reaffirm, that music renews in me my thankfulness for God's gifts of creation which he has given to us – to each of us – in some form. And music focuses for me the creative gifts of God in people like ourselves.

The second point I want to make about faith and music is that music is another language: which God has given us to enable us to interpret and comment upon the world which we inhabit and experience – with all its mysteries.

I'm not surprised at the enduring popularity of the radio programme, *Desert Island Discs*. You don't need me to describe it in detail. A few weeks ago, it was the singer Thomas Allen who was envisaging that remote possibility of shipwreck. I was particularly interested in his choice. I happen to know well the mining village in County Durham – Seaham – where he was born and brought up, in very humble circumstances. He was a chapel-goer in his earliest years. I also knew one of his singing teachers in London – Meriel St Claire – and helped at her funeral.

Tom Allen is in his late fifties now. He's sung at Covent Garden and

Glyndebourne. Maybe he's sung here at your Festival. In his selection of records for his time alone on that mythical desert island, he said he would certainly want one record from Bach's *St John Passion*. He chose the 30-year-old recording conducted by Benjamin Britten, at Alde-burgh, with Peter Pears as the Evangelist and Gwynne Howell as Jesus. The Evangelist describes Jesus going with his disciples to the Garden of Gethsemane. There Judas brings a band of men, with torches and weapons. Jesus simply asks: 'Whom seek ye?' They answer 'Jesus of Nazareth.' And Jesus says 'I am he.'

Then the chorus sings one of Bach's most marvellous chorales:

> O generous love
> O vast and deep compassion
> That brings thee now
> To thy most bitter passion.

Tom Allen said that whatever that island was, and whatever life was like on it, he would need to listen to that record: for nothing in his experience made a more profound comment on existence and life – on its pain, and evil, but also on its underlying purpose.

Of course, it's not the music alone in the *St John Passion* that provides us with a language to interpret life and the world wherever we are – it's music perfectly suited to the words, to describing a particular action – which paradoxically we call The Passion of Jesus.

And there's a third aspect of the subject of faith and music to which I want to draw your attention this morning, and that's beauty. There are various ways in which beauty in music may be revealed – vocally, in soloists; in Tom Allen; in choirs; instrumentally, by soloists like Bren-del; by composers; and most of us, whether or not we're musicians, have some kind of love for beauty in music. We may differ in our choice of music, but few of us would want to deny the existence of beauty in music.

The great Russian philosopher and theologian, Nicolas Berdyaev, wrote: 'Every bit of beauty in this world, the beauty of man, of nature, of a work of art, is a partial transfiguration of this world, a creative breakthrough to another.'

Dr Olive Wyon wrote:

> The wonder of Creation suggests another gateway to worship; the door of Beauty. Whatever kind of beauty stirs us, to delight or painful longing, we can use as a ladder to rise above ourselves. For this love of beauty is divinely implanted. The touch of beauty when we feel it, is not to be merely a passing delight: it is the call of God, inviting us gently and sweetly to turn to him.

The beauty of music is the call of God.

So: Music and creation. Music as a language to interpret the world. Music as the call of God – through its beauty.

And a fourth point.

Music always involves the use of our bodies – to make sounds as a singer, or as instrumentalists. But although it involves very down-to-earth use of our bodies – like five-finger exercises – it doesn't end with the down-to-earth body; it employs it as a vehicle that helps us to get to heaven. And it reminds us that we were created for heaven.

It's through our bodies that we experience emotion aroused by music. The word 'body' is sometimes used in relation to an individual – and sometimes to a group of people – like a choir or an orchestra: a body of people. Choirs and orchestras remind us just what a 'body of people' can achieve together. So it's not surprising that St Paul calls the Church 'the Body of Christ'. Music, in other words, gives us a vision of what we were meant to be and do, both individually and together.

Before I end, let me share with you just a thought or two on music and time. People have written volumes on the subject. Only recently, Jeremy Begbie, a Cambridge theologian and musician, has written a profound study: *Theology, Music and Time.*

Every musician understands something about time. Rhythm is to do with time. Time is essential to music. It's part of the raw material of music; and yet, often, by employing time, it gives us a vision of what is beyond time.

How shall I illustrate that? Well, I could give a thousand examples of time and music – they're inseparable. But since I'm coming to the end of what I have to say, may I suggest we think of the last chorus of Handel's *Messiah*. It's, of course, only one word – AMEN. Yet the rhythm of the fugue, that the musical genius of Handel creates, transports us to another world. And so it is with every great composition. Time is of the essence – to take us beyond time.

Let me add one more quotation, from a great musician: an organist, who knew more about the works of Bach than almost any other writer; a theologian; a philosopher; but also a great medical missionary, with his own hospital in French Equatorial Africa: Albert Schweitzer. He wrote of Johann Sebastian Bach:

> The unique thing about Bach is precisely the fact that he made no effort to win recognition for his greatest works, and did not summon the world to make acquaintance with them. Hence the kind of consecration that rests upon his works. They discourse to us of something that will be imperishable, simply because it is big and true, something that was written, not to win recognition, but because it had to come out of him. Bach himself was apparently not conscious of the extraordinary greatness of his work. He never dreamed that his works alone, not those of the men around him, would remain visible to the coming generation.

Perhaps that's another characteristic of great music and of the great musician – a kind of consecration.

Music does not let time intimidate us. It employs it to the glory of God – a song, a hymn, a *Sanctus*, a Week's Festival: music employs time to take us beyond time.

The last words Shakespeare puts on the lips of the dying Hamlet are: 'The rest is silence'. In thinking about faith and music – and time – it's worth saying at the end: 'The rest is silence'. Rests in music are very important. The rest in music is, of course, silence. Silence in relation to music is very important. We must never think we can plumb the mystery of music, however much we analyse it. What music *is* will always be something of a mystery. That's why it's such a good vehicle for speaking about God. It can do so much – and so can we. But 'the rest is silence'.

Let's be silent now.

6 Remembrance Day: Westminster Abbey, 11 November 2001

I said, when I welcomed you at the beginning of this service, that a number of you will have come here tonight because today is Remembrance Day and Westminster Abbey is where, for over 80 years now, the Tomb of the Unknown Warrior is to be found. It confronts us, of course, immediately we enter the Abbey.

For both those who have come here tonight because of the Tomb of the Unknown Warrior and for those who may have been unaware of the Tomb's existence, I think it may help to tell you again – in some detail – just how the Tomb of the Unknown Warrior came to be placed here. It was, of course, after the end of the First World War – the 'Great War', as it was called for many years, until the Second World War. And it's important to remind ourselves just how great and terrible a war that First World War was.

The losers in that war lost three and a half million soldiers on the battlefield. The victors lost five million one hundred thousand men.

The number of war dead for the different countries involved was:

Germany	1,800,000
Russia	1,700,000
France	1,384,000
Austro-Hungary	1,290,000
Britain	743,000
Italy	615,000

Canada	60,000
Australia	59,000
India	49,000
United States	48,000
New Zealand	16,000
South Africa	8,000

On average, this was more than 5,600 soldiers killed on each day of the four years of the war.

In other words, what happened in the United States on September 11th this year, happened every day for over four years.

On the first day of the Battle of the Somme 20,000 British soldiers were killed. It's facts like these which I think made Remembrance Day – from its inception – so important and so powerful to so many.

In 1920, the year after the Armistice, an army chaplain, David Railton, suggested to the Dean of Westminster, Dean Ryle, that an unknown soldier should be buried here in the Abbey, among the great leaders of the nation. In 1916, Railton had noticed a grave with the pencilled inscription on a wooden cross, 'An Unknown Soldier of the Black Watch'. A committee under Lord Curzon recommended that an unknown soldier should be disinterred in France; the King – King George V – at first disliked the idea. The soldier was to be called the 'Unknown Warrior', so that he might represent all who had been killed, whether as soldiers, sailors or airmen. Four bodies were brought from the main battle areas to a chapel at St Pol. There, one body was selected at midnight between 7 and 8 November. A destroyer carried the coffin to Dover. On board were six barrels of earth for the burial, from the Ypres Salient, so that the body should rest in the soil on which so many English troops had been killed. The coffin was draped with the Union Jack which Railton had frequently used as an altar and coffin covering in France.

On 11 November 1920, the King, after unveiling the new Cenotaph in Whitehall, walked behind the gun carriage which bore the coffin to the Abbey. The appropriateness and impressiveness of the ceremony removed the initial apprehensions which the King had felt. The Prayer Book Burial Service followed. C. F. G. Masterman, a Liberal Party politician, who disliked the romantic language used about the Unknown Warrior, nevertheless commented: 'We are burying every boy's father, and every woman's lover, and every mother's child.'

The whole concept was carried out at each stage with elaborate ceremony – for example, the selection by a blindfolded officer of one of the bodies at midnight in a guarded chapel – illustrated the way in which the desire for Remembrance moved the nation towards a nationally, and even internationally, accepted symbolism and ritual, for the process was subsequently followed in several other countries.

The texts on the tomb were invariably biblical:

'Greater Love hath no man than this'
'Unknown yet well known'
'Dying and behold we live'
'The Lord knoweth them that are his'.

These were chosen by the Dean of Westminster from the wreaths laid a year before.

In 1931, David Railton wrote further thoughts about the significance of the Unknown Soldier, whom Railton would have preferred to have been called 'The Unknown Comrade'. 'People,' he said, 'learn the unity of all types of men at that grave. They see that in the long run, all men of goodwill are comrades in Life, Death and the Hereafter.'

What I have said so far does not form a *sermon* for Remembrance Day – even though what I have said I regard as very important for visitors to Westminster Abbey to hear and know – and not only *visitors* to the Abbey. A sermon only becomes a sermon when we ask what God is doing and what God is saying to us in the present in and through particular events – if we have ears to hear and eyes to see. And I think

God has several things to say to us on what we in England call Remembrance Day in 'The Year of Our Lord 2001'.

First: I think He wants us to hear Him say something to us about Memory and Remembrance. The marvel and mystery of memory is one of the great wonders of our humanity. The poet Shelley wrote:

> Music when soft voices die
> Vibrates in the memory.

But it's not only music that vibrates there. Our childhood memories often last a lifetime, and are unique to us. So are many of our memories. In other words: our individual identities are bound up with our memories – good and bad; pleasant and painful. Remembrance and identity go together. What we remember makes us who we are.

And one of the questions that press upon us as soon as we start to ponder the mystery of memory is: 'How can we purge our memories? Indeed: can they be purged?' Forgiveness is not simply forgetting – even if that were possible. As a priest, I often have people come to me who say, 'I just can't forget what he or she or they have done – or what I have done.' So the gift of memory and the gift of forgiveness need to go together.

If remembrance is only the recalling of tragedy, that is terrible.

But remembrance of time-past most often contains some lessons for the future. And even the remembrance of the most terrible events of the past often contains, at one and the same time, memories of things for which we can only be thankful: for instance, the bravery, courage, comradeship and self-sacrifice of war. Memory of sacrifice often breeds hope – fresh faith and hope – that the deeds that were done were not in vain.

I think any *sermon* on Remembrance Day must aim at helping all who hear it to reflect afresh on the mystery of memory – in thanksgiving, and penitence, and faith, and hope.

We become more the persons we were meant to be when we explore the heights and depths of our memories. And that is true whatever our nationality, race, or religion. It is true of all humanity.

But I don't think I want to end my sermon there.

I think I'd want to think aloud on what God has to say to us not only about memory and remembrance but about that word 'Unknown'.

When we remember somebody, we usually remember something about them that we've known – their voice; their hair; their looks; their walk. To remember someone *Unknown* is quite a demand. How do we think of someone Unknown?

One of the poets of the Great War, Charles Sorley – the cousin of the politician 'RAB' Butler – wrote a poem that was found in his kit-bag when it was sent home from France in 1916 after his death.

> When you see millions of the mouthless dead
> Across your dreams in pale battalions go,
> Say not soft things as other men have said,
> That you'll remember. For you need not so.
> Give them not praise. For, deaf, how should they know
> It is not curses heaped on each gashed head?
> Nor tears. Their blind eyes see not your tears flow.
> Nor honour. It is easy to be dead.
> Say only this, 'They are dead'. Then add thereto,
> 'Yet many a better one has died before'.
> Then, scanning all the o'ercrowded mass, should you
> Perceive one face that you loved heretofore,
> It is a spook. None wears the face you knew.
> Great Death has made all his for evermore.

One can only sympathize with that bitter and angry cynicism, expressed amid all the carnage which killed so many, including Sorley himself. Yet, I think, in the end, that poem, that scream, presses upon us the ultimate and unavoidable question, which St Paul answered in his phrase 'Unknown yet well known'. We are all in the end either despatched into oblivion – as clearly Sorley believed – or accepted in the Beloved.

The answer of faith is that we are known to God our creator, and loved by God our creator and redeemer.

Richard Baxter, the seventeenth-century Puritan Divine, wrote a poem which expresses that faith – which I confess thankfully is my faith:

> Christ who knows all his sheep
>   Will all in safety keep,
> He will not lose one soul,
>   Nor ever fail us;
> Nor we the promised goal,
>   Though hell assail us.
>
> I know my God is just;
> To him I wholly trust
>   All that I have and am,
>   All that I hope for:
> All's sure and seen to him,
>   Which here I grope for.
>
> Lord Jesus, take this spirit:
> We trust thy love and merit.
>   Take home the wandering sheep,
>   For thou hast sought it;
> This soul in safety keep,
>   For thou hast bought it.

In the end, Christian affirmation is that the Unknown Warrior is well known – to God.

7 Christian Hope: The Chapel Royal, St James's Palace, 30 December 2001

It was on the last Sunday of last year that I was privileged to preach in this Chapel on 'Christian Hope'. For many, this last year has, in fact, been another *annus horribilis* – and, of course, particularly in the United States. So what am I to take as my subject today? This last Sunday of this year? I'm sure I must take that same subject again: 'Christian Hope'.

And I do that 'new inspired' by that wonderful passage we had for our first lesson this morning – from the prophet Isaiah:

> The wilderness and the solitary place shall be
> glad . . . and the desert shall rejoice and blossom as the rose.

However, I will confess to you that, at home, I have a particularly precious possession. It's a CD of Winchester Cathedral Choir singing Samuel Sebastian Wesley's sublime setting of those words, which he wrote as an anthem for the opening of the new organ of Hereford Cathedral, in 1832. And sometimes, when I have cause to be – let's say 'down in the dumps' – I put on that record, and hear those words again, and receive again Isaiah's instruction: 'Say to them of a fearful heart: Be strong; fear not . . .'.

But S. S. Wesley's setting is not only of those first six verses of Isaiah

35 – which formed our lesson this morning – it goes on to include four more verses, ending with:

> And the ransomed of the Lord shall return
> and come to Zion with songs and everlasting joy...

I myself think those four verses are essential to the understanding of the first six. For they make it clear that Isaiah's promise that 'the desert shall blossom as the rose' is, for the most part, allegorical and metaphorical. It's a vision of heaven.

This particular year – when we may be tempted to think of this worldly wilderness – and the deserts, for instance, of Afghanistan – or the desert now in New York, where the two towers stood – it's of huge importance for our eyes to be lifted to 'another world than this', and for our vision of the Christian Hope to be transcendent. St Paul's words of wisdom in his First Letter to the Corinthians have never been more important: 'If in this life only we have hope in Christ, we are of all men most miserable.'

But, I hasten to say, Christian Hope does not run away from this world. Indeed, since 11th September, I have been trying to think afresh, to confront afresh, what the Christian Gospel has to say about the world we live in now.

And I suppose it's not all that surprising that it has been the great American theologian and political philosopher, Reinhold Niebuhr, who has come to my rescue. One of Niebuhr's best books was simply called *Beyond Tragedy*. Niebuhr makes you see that the long drama of human history – with its unending conflict between good and evil – could never be resolved this side of the coming of God's kingdom.

Moral Man in Immoral Society was the title of another of Niebuhr's great works – in which he pleaded that we should never underestimate the degree and persistence of human corruption – not simply in, say, terrorists and fanatics, but in us all – as individuals, and groupings, and nations. It is utopian to expect peace and prosperity in our world and in our time: which is why fanatics make a smash and grab raid on it. Niebuhr said that 'the sad job of politics is to bring justice to a sinful world' – and he expected to see sin in the structures of American society – not just in the societies outside America, though I was privileged to hear him in Central Hall, Westminster, when I was a student, some years ago!, brilliantly analysing the sins of our society. He talked on the necessity of compromise ethics as well as ideals. He said that, 'Nothing worth doing is completed in our lifetime; therefore we must be saved by hope.'

Which causes me to say that, as one gets older, one is bound to realize that peace and prosperity are a mirage for most of humanity: a mirage we must go on living with.

Many of us will have heard and seen, only a fortnight ago, on television, this year's Richard Dimbleby Lecture – delivered – and delivered powerfully – by the former President of the United States, Bill Clinton. It was both intelligent and intelligible. It was both thought-provoking and full of hope. My only criticism of it was that it was not only hopeful but optimistic. It did not take Reinhold Niebuhr's dictum sufficiently seriously, that:

> Not much evil is done by evil people.
> Most of the evil is done by good people who do not know that
> they are not good.

The evil of the terrorists is obvious. The evil of us ordinary mortals, less so.

Then, what is Christian Hope?

It's that while we pray 'Thy Kingdom come on earth as it is in heaven', we must expect to enjoy that Kingdom in its fullness beyond this world – for life on this earth is extraordinarily brief. And the saying is all too true that 'All men think all men mortal – but themselves.'

It's peculiarly appropriate that I should use the words of an American theologian to stir up within us today the virtue of Christian Hope.

Niebuhr said: 'All men who live with any degree of serenity live by some assurance of grace.'

His best-known prayer was: 'God give us grace to accept with serenity the things that cannot be changed, courage to change the things that should be changed, and the wisdom to distinguish the one from the other.'

That, I believe, is the way to tread the paths of Christian Hope – into this New Year.

8 The Soper sermon: Soper, Simeon and the Spirituality of Ageing: The West London Methodist Mission, Hinde Street, 27 January 2002

I accepted with alacrity, and with great pleasure, your kind invitation to preach this morning this year's Soper Sermon.

I accepted it as, of course, an honour – but also as the chance to discharge something of my debt to Lord Soper – outstanding for many years. I accepted it also because I saw immediately a subject which I thought would be after Donald's heart – at least towards the end of his life: 'Soper, Simeon, and the Spirituality of Ageing'.

But let me begin by telling you, briefly, how and why Donald Soper came to mean so much to me. I was brought up as a Methodist for my first five years – in Chadwell Heath: ten miles east of Bow Bells. My Presbyterian parents had moved from Camden Town, when I, their fourth child, arrived; and the Methodist 'tin tabernacle' in Chadwell Heath, became for them the next best thing to what Somers Town Presbyterian Church had been.

I owe a huge amount to my Methodist Sunday-schooling. It was Mrs Hasler, the superintendent, who told us to 'close your peepers' when we were saying our prayers. *Hushed was the evening hymn* is still one of my favourite hymns, because I learnt it in Sunday School.

When people ask me why I'm Church of England, the simple answer is: ' 'Cos the Methodist Church closed down!' – and I became a Church of England choirboy.

Donald Soper came into my life only when I was 14 – that's to say: in 1939. When the war broke out, my father decided I should not be evacuated with my school – Dagenham County High – but go out to work.

That year I started as an office boy, at a Norwegian shipping firm, in Mark Lane, in the City, not far from Tower Hill. And, whatever jobs I did, for the next seven years – a Thamesside wharf by London Bridge, after the Norwegian invasion had closed down my shipping firm: and a wharf on the South Bank, where the Globe Theatre now stands, after the London Bridge wharf had been destroyed in the 'blitz' in September 1940 – wherever I worked, Wednesdays at Tower Hill, and listening to Donald – and learning from him – became a regular part of my life, for, as I say, seven years.

I doubt whether I could have had a better tutor in public preaching; or in evangelism; or in the pastoral response to the enquirer; or in perceiving the hollowness of the insincere enquirer; or in humour and evangelism; or in Christian socialism – and the Church in politics; or in Christian pacifism; or in Christian action in general.

Donald on Tower Hill was, literally, my Open University.

And little did I realize that I should begin my ministry as a vicar in Camberwell – in 1959 – next to where Donald had begun his ministry – in Oakley Place, just off the Old Kent Road; and that when later, I became Director of Christian Action – in succession to Canon Collins – I should find myself working at so much in which Donald had been intimately involved for years.

But now I must proceed to the subject which I have said would be 'after Donald's heart' – 'Simeon and the Spirituality of Ageing'. Next Saturday, many Christians will be keeping Candlemas or 'The Presentation of Christ in the Temple'. It has, of course, been the subject of several great works of art; and Luke himself tells the story with the consummate skill of a great artist in words.

That story would recall to any devout Jew the dedication of the child Samuel. Simeon, whoever else he was, was a devout Jew – eagerly waiting for the Messiah. The Holy Spirit had kindled in him a flame of devotion and expectancy; and when Jesus' parents brought Him to the temple, Luke records that Simeon said what we now know as one of the greatest Christian canticles: the *Nunc Dimittis*: 'Lord, now lettest thou thy servant depart in peace . . . Mine eyes have seen thy salvation.'

The word used there for 'depart' – 'depart in peace' – is the same as that for the freeing of a slave. Some of the *Nunc Dimittis* is a direct quotation from the prophet Isaiah. It's also quite possible for the words to be translated: 'Lord, now let your servant *retire* in peace.'

With Simeon was the 84-year-old Anna. She, too, voiced her thanks to God. I think you will see why I regard this scene as a kind of icon – a biblical icon – that can be a beacon in the spiritual life of each one of us, and, particularly, to those of us who are ageing.

Let me put it this way: I think there's a *Nunc Dimittis* to be articulated – at some time – in and from us all. It will be different for each one of us.

Let me make one or two comments and suggestions. Some people nowadays describe the final stages of life as the 'third and fourth ages' – when we've retired.

It's not all that surprising that we all need to ask the Holy Spirit afresh to enflame us to a new pattern of devotion appropriate to our age. I've found that carefully compiling – in part, re-writing – my own personal prayer book – my loose-leaf prayer book – has been, at this stage, very rewarding. It has several '*Nunc Dimittis*' in it now which are specially appropriate to my years!

I don't want to give you too many examples, because your prayer book must be *your* prayer book. But I have inserted into my prayer book this year a hymn – a *Nunc Dimittis* – which was in the Methodist Hymn Book which was given me – I'm thankful to say – by the Methodist undergraduates at Trinity College, Cambridge, in June 1959, when I was their chaplain but I never noticed it then!

Let me read it to you now. Now it says exactly what I want to say – and sing:

MHB 78

How shall I sing that majesty
   Which angels do admire?
Let dust in dust and silence lie;
   Sing, sing, ye heavenly choir.
Thousands of thousands stand around
   Thy throne, O God most high;
Ten thousand times ten thousand sound
   Thy praise; but who am I?

Thy brightness unto them appears;
   Whilst I Thy footsteps trace
A sound of God comes to my ears,
   But they behold Thy face.
They sing because Thou art their Sun;
   Lord, send a beam on me;
For where heaven is but once begun
   There alleluias be.

Enlighten with faith's light my heart,
   Inflame it with love's fire;
Then shall I sing and bear a part
   With that celestial choir.

I shall, I fear, be dark and cold,
   With all my fire and light;
Yet when Thou does accept their gold,
   Lord, treasure up my mite.

How great a being, Lord, is Thine,
   Which doth all beings keep!
Thy knowledge is the only line
   To sound so vast a deep.
Thou art a sea without a shore,
   A sun without a sphere;
Thy time is now and evermore,
   Thy place is every where.

That hymn, of the seventeenth-century Divine, John Mason, is now part of my *Nunc Dimittis*.

First, then, let your re-writing of your own prayer book articulate your own *Nunc Dimittis*. Secondly, it's my experience that at my age I have been suddenly hit by bereavement – of a kind for which no one prepared me. So many of my contemporaries are taken seriously ill, and so many of them have, in fact, died – and I have to go to their funerals and memorial services, and, indeed, conduct them in my 'retirement', so-called. And no one told me it would be like this!

Whatever else I've retired from, one thing is clear: I have not retired from bereavement! And I need a spirituality that will enable me to say: 'Lord, now lettest Thou thy servant depart in peace' to every one of my friends who leaves this world. And their death makes it clear that I need to prepare myself to 'depart in peace'.

Very recently, I came across a marvellous booklet on *Older People and Bereavement*, published by Methodist Homes for the Aged, in co-operation with the Christian Council for Ageing. It's by Sydney Callaghan. And I can't imagine a better booklet for its purpose.

That booklet led me to a whole series of Halley Stewart booklets, each one of which has something to contribute, not only to our *Nunc Dimittis*, but to helping us to help others to articulate their *Nunc Dimittis*.

Let me just read their titles:

Spirituality in the Later Years of Life
Adapting our Lifestyle in Retirement
The Ageing Single Person
Ageing in a Strange Land
Facing Terminal Illness
The Spiritual Needs of People with Dementia
A Future Home
Those who Care for Others

And

The Church's Ministry to Ageing People.

I ask myself: 'Could there be a more helpful series?' And I'm grateful that the Project Editor, Albert Jewell, has done such a good job.

I hope you are beginning to be convinced – if you need any convincing – that the phrase 'Lord, now release thy servant' has many helpful resonances and meanings. I can sit in my chair, in silence, and say to God: 'Release me from fear and anxiety'; 'Release me from the kind of attachment that makes all thought of leaving this world beyond me'; 'Mine eyes have seen your salvation . . .'; 'Help me to trust that Love which is Salvation . . .'; 'Be Thou my vision.'

Of course, sometimes in old age it will be difficult to distinguish our *Nunc Dimittis* from Christ's prayer: 'My God, my God, why hast Thou forsaken me?'

I don't suggest that all the prayer of the ageing should be self-concerned. (Donald would never have approved of that!) Nor will our prayer ever be only self-concerned if it's concerned with the Love that is Salvation. Nor will it be pietistic. I can't imagine the prayer of Donald without passionate and committed prayer for the peace of the world.

I did not mention to you the Centre for Spirituality of Ageing, which is run by Methodist Homes for the Aged, in Yorkshire, near Headingley; and I want to do so, because it takes very seriously the arts and crafts; and I think they can play an important part in our *Nunc Dimittis*. I have several friends who have taken up painting in retirement, and their painting contributes a great deal to their *Nunc Dimittis*. Others have started writing poetry in their ageing years, and have discovered the joy of words, so that their *Nunc Dimittis* is almost as beautifully expressed as St Luke's.

There is a kind of fellowship in the *Nunc Dimittis* – all of us learning to say it, in our later years, with a new sincerity and depth.

How shall I bring my 'Soper Sermon' to an end?

I want to mention thankfully Donald's courage – on Tower Hill and in Hyde Park; and on platform upon platform – in peacemaking as well as preaching. And I suggest that Donald's courage has something to say to us all as we articulate our Simeon-like *Nunc Dimittis*.

Sometimes when we're ageing it's the day ahead that will take courage. Sometimes, it's the night ahead.

My mentor and friend, Eric Abbott, who became Dean of Westminster, on the day he was ordained was very frightened of all that lay ahead. His 'digs' as a curate looked out on the Thames by the Tate Gallery. He pulled the curtains before he got down on his knees to say his prayers – that first evening of his ministry – and looked out across the river. There, flashing every few seconds, was a red neon sign: 'COURAGE! COURAGE! COURAGE!' He remembered that sign – which, of course, came from a brewery! – all the years of his ministry.

I always associate Donald with the Methodist Sacramental Fellowship, founded in 1935. So I shall conclude with a prayer, which I have in my loose-leaf prayer book – a prayer written fairly recently for the Holy Communion Service: a prayer which never fails to open my eyes again to 'Thy Salvation' – 'Which Thou hast prepared before the face of all people'. In other words: it's an important part of my *Nunc Dimittis*; and I commend it to you, in thankful remembrance of Donald Soper:

> Father of all:
>> We give you thanks and praise,
>> that when we were still far off
>> you met us in your Son and brought us home.
> Dying and living.
>> he declared your love,
>> gave us grace,
>> and opened the gate of glory,
> May we who share Christ's Body
>> live his risen life;
> We who drink his cup
>> bring life to others;

We whom the Spirit lights
   give light to the world.
Keep us firm in the hope you have set before us,
   so we and all your children shall be free,
   and the whole earth live to praise your name;
   through Jesus Christ our Lord. Amen.

9 A lamb to the slaughter: St Mary Abbots', Kensington, 17 February 2002

> I was like a gentle lamb that is led to the slaughter.
>
> (Jeremiah: Chapter 11, verse 19)

Our Old Testament lesson this morning came from the Book of the Prophet Jeremiah; and I want to do what I can to 'bring him back alive' – so to speak – this first Sunday of Lent. And I don't think there's a better verse to do that than: 'I was like a gentle lamb that is led to the slaughter.'

Some of you will, no doubt, have read a book written a century and more ago, by the mid-Victorian writer Richard Jefferies: *The Story of My Heart*. If one were to give a title to the Book of the Prophet Jeremiah, I doubt whether one could do better than *The Story of My Heart*; for Jeremiah is the story of a heart that was broken many times, but which had, by the end, come to know the heights of faith that tower above despair.

If Kensington were Jerusalem, Jeremiah would have been born in, say, Hampstead. And for 19 years he would have lived there. The birds, and trees, and flowers, and all the country around would have been in some way for him the clothing of eternity: for to Jeremiah, as to no other prophet, the world of nature was the world that spoke to him of the Lord.

But his heart was seldom happy. Five miles away was the Holy City. And through all his childhood Jerusalem was as Babylon: the home of the rich and powerful, and of the miserable and poor. He prayed for the peace of Jerusalem. The temple was to him the centre of a hollow religion. The smoke of sacrifice never ceased to ascend from its altars: but there were few hearts offered to God. There was extreme social injustice and flagrant religious abuse; and all alike were content to have it so – king and countrymen and priests. And, as Jeremiah grew in wisdom and stature, a great anger and indignation grew in his heart for the things which were happening within the 'Holy City'.

But Jeremiah was not born of the stuff of which prophets are made. A 'gentle lamb' does not make a fiery prophet. And this hesitant youth, brought up in a pious home, knowing so well what the Lord required of him, by nature shrank from what he must say and do.

The Voice of the Lord seemed to be saying strange things to him – within him:

> Before I formed thee in the womb I knew thee,
> And before thou camest forth I set thee apart;
> A prophet to the nations I ordained thee.

And Jeremiah answered, talking to himself yet knowing he was not simply talking to himself:

> 'Ah, my Lord God
> Behold I know not how to speak
> For I am but a lad.'

> 'Say not thou art a lad' the Lord seemed to answer:
> 'For to whomsoever I send thee thou shalt go;
> And whatsoever I command thee thou shalt speak.
> Have no fear before them: for I am with thee for thy succour.'

And it was as if the Lord had stretched forth his hand and laid it on Jeremiah's mouth; and he heard the Lord say:

'Lo, I put my word within thy mouth.
See: I put thee in charge this day –
Over the nations and over the kingdoms –
To pluck up and to pull down, to build and to plant.'

Whatever work this young man had to do, one thing was certain – he would not do it of his own power. This shy, retiring lad could only leave the shelter of his own country home, to speak within the city, and live in the limelight of the nation's life, because he believed God's spirit was upon him – God's word, literally within him.

So within the temple court, and at the city gate, he stood and spoke the word of God – as a man possessed. It was as if in 1939 someone had stood on the steps of St Paul's and prophesied that Hitler would defeat us – because of our sins: our personal and our social sins.

And, of course, no one listened.

He said Assyria would destroy Jerusalem if they did not listen to his words. But no one heard. They put in hand a reformation of their worship's most flagrant evils; but to Jeremiah it was nothing. Their ritual was changed: their liturgy was revised: their hearts were just the same. So Jeremiah preached on: 'Jerusalem will fall.'

Everyone turned against him. His fellow citizens forsook him and disowned him. He had no friend to comfort him. He had no wife – he saw it as God's will that he should be alone. But, worst of all, it seemed the *Lord* had left him; for though he prophesied Jerusalem's fall, it was Assyria that fell.

For 20 years he'd tried to preach the Word of God; but it had come to nothing. He could not understand. He had not prophesied from arrogance. He spoke only because he believed God commanded him. It was the word of God. Had he not pleaded that he could not speak?

Even upon his countrymen, whom his words condemned – his heart poured forth love and pity.

The gentle lamb was led very close to the slaughter.

'Cursed be the day that I was born' he cried out –

50

'The day my mother bore me,
Be it unblessed.

Cursed be the man who brought my Father the news
"A man child has been born,"
Making him glad.

Why came I forth from the womb
To see this trouble and sorrow
And to consume my days in shame?'

'WHY?'... That was the cry from the stricken lamb: from Jeremiah's deep heart's core.

He could not see then beyond disillusion. He could not see what that agony of wrestling was doing to him – changing him from the timid, frightened young man: from simply the impassioned prophet – into a man of profound strength and patience.

The raw material of his early confidence in God was changed into the finished product of faith – tenacious faith – and love, and disciplined humility. From this humbling to the dust there arose a reborn Jeremiah.

In Judah, king followed king – good and bad. The city was the same: rotten to the core. And Jeremiah's words were now fulfilled. For though Assyria was no more, the Babylonians took their place; and now Jerusalem fell; and many families were carted off to Babylon.

Some of you present this morning are old enough to have seen a tyrant Germany fall, only for a tyrant Russia to succeed, and march off hordes of captives to a distant land.

It is to a fallen Jerusalem and to those distant exiles that the reborn Jeremiah speaks – and when he cannot speak, his friend of those later years, Baruch, goes to the temple courts and speaks what Jeremiah would have said. 'There are false prophets right at the heart of Jerusalem: at the centre of the nations and the church's life.' They say: 'There's no problem. There will be peace – the exiles quick return.'

Jeremiah cannot stomach their glib and easy words.

'They heal the sin of my people lightly, saying: Peace, Peace, where there is no peace.'

Jeremiah was imprisoned as a traitor, flogged, then thrown down a deep well, and left to die. Jerusalem was utterly destroyed. The king was killed; then Jeremiah was dragged off, unwillingly – to Egypt – by his fellow countrymen. So ends the story of his heart. So ends his life, his work – some would have said 'in vain'.

Yet in his last years we do not see a Jeremiah plunged in despair. We see a man whose confidence is in the grand design of God. Jeremiah goes to his death quite sure that God will raise His Israel in his own good time. The gentle lamb is led with faith, blind faith, to the slaughter.

Jeremiah is placed right at the beginning of our readings for Lent because he foreshadows the Lamb of God, the Christ of God, who 'learned obedience through the things he suffered'. Jeremiah foreshadowed the prophet of God who preached within the temple courts: who said: 'My house shall be called a house of prayer but you have made it a den of robbers.'

Jeremiah foreshadowed the Christ who cried out 'My God, my God, why? . . .'

Jeremiah foreshadowed the Christ, and many a Christian in the centuries before Christ. I have on my shelves half a dozen books at least concerning those 'gentle lambs' who were led to the slaughter before, and during, the Second World War – like Dietrich Bonhoeffer.

It was Jeremiah relating his faith to the events of his day – the political and social and religious events of his day – which led him to the slaughter. What, I wonder, has that to say to us today?

We are awaiting, at the moment, the appointment of a new Archbishop of Canterbury. The Committee who will make recommendations need, of course, our prayers this Lent. I myself hope they will recommend not simply 'a safe pair of hands'. (My God! We need more than that!) I hope they will recommend a prophet!

It was my privilege to be Director for 17 years of an organization called *Christian Action* – founded by Canon Collins in Oxford Town Hall in 1946. On his tombstone in St Paul's, it says:

> He worked for reconciliation between nations and races, and helped those who were deprived, persecuted, imprisoned and exiled. He founded and directed Christian Action, International Defence and Aid for Southern Africa, and, with others, the Campaign for Nuclear Disarmament.

As Canon Collins' successor, I was privileged to be the one who proposed to Robert Runcie, Archbishop of Canterbury, that he should set up an Archbishop's Commission on Urban Priority Areas, which, praise God, he did; and the result was the Report *Faith in the City* and The Church Urban Fund.

The man who chaired that Commission – and the man who chaired the Committee which chose Robert Runcie to be Archbishop of Canterbury – Sir Richard O'Brien – is on your sick list today. His eighty-second birthday was last Friday.

I have no doubt whatever that the Archbishop we need now must stand before the nation and continue to trumpet the needs of the Urban Priority Areas in this country – and of the poverty-stricken areas of the world. We need to give, for instance, the peoples of Africa hope and justice. (How dare they say that Tony Blair should not have flown off to Africa!) But it is not only Africa that has to be in our hearts and minds. We need a prophet who will lead us into a more profound dialogue with other faiths than ours.

The Church of England needs now a prophet who will proclaim what Christ proclaimed: 'Inasmuch as ye have done it unto the least of these my brethren, ye have done it unto me.' Such a prophet will no doubt be led to the slaughter – as Jeremiah was. As Jesus was. And yet – in the end – Jesus the prophet was 'the safe pair of hands' – the saving pair of hands – the Saviour of the World: the Saviour of you and me.

10 All you need is Love: St Saviour's, Pimlico, 9 June 2002

This last week of the Queen's Jubilee has been unforgettable for us all. I look back now to last Monday afternoon – when I was lying on my bed, watching on TV the Queen launching the Jubilee celebrations in Slough, with the school children – of many races – sing *All you need is Love*. It was a marvellous beginning. And that theme was taken up again and again, across the country, during the week.

And I want to say, first of all, how glad I am that that particular phrase, and that particular song, has been sung as a kind of theme song of the Jubilee. *All you need is Love*. That's, of course, true. All I need is Love, and all you need is Love. But I think everyone who take those words on their lips needs to think just what Love is. And if the Jubilee were to lead people to thinking what Love is: that would be marvellous.

There are, of course, many different forms of Love – stretching from the romantic to the self-sacrificial.

There's a warning in the writings of someone who's often read these days at weddings – Kahil Gibran – who wrote a book called *The Prophet*. In that book he wrote: 'For even as love crowns you, so shall he crucify you. Even as he is for your growth, so he is for your pruning.'

So where should we start our thinking about Love – if 'All we need is Love'? I think the best place for Christians – but not only Christians – to start is with St John's simple statement in his Epistle, when he says:

Beloved, let us love one another,
   for love is of God;
   and he who loves is born of God
      and knows God.
   He who does not love does not know God, for
      God is Love.

If God is love, and we are created by God – and who else can we be created by? – then to love is to return to our roots in God.

We can, of course, do that in prayer. And our prayer can often best begin by simply reminding ourselves that the loving God is our creator: the source of all our being. And that prayer can take place anywhere – at any time. But it needs to take place at specific times if it is to take place at all.

God is love – and we have been created by Love – for Love. That's the purpose of our whole being.

There are certain sayings about Love which I've come to value highly over the years. For instance: William Blake – the English poet and painter and mystic – who lived across the river in Lambeth – wrote, of course, *Jerusalem* – which has been sung several times by the crowds this last week. Blake wrote two lines about love which have stuck with me ever since I first heard them: 'He who would do good to another must do it in Minute Particulars. General good is the plea of the scoundrel, the hypocrite and the flatterer.' He might have said: 'He who would love another must do it in Minute Particulars' – not simply in some vague and general emotion.

Last night, on the radio, there was a remarkable programme that told the story of Thalidomide and its victims. If you were born – as a result of Thalidomide – with no arms or legs, 'All you need is Love'. But you would need love that thought in detail – in minute particulars.

And that brings me to a second favourite saying of mine – which comes from another hero of mine – C. F. Andrews – 'Charlie'Andrews. He's been a hero of mine for at least 50 years. Charlie Andrews worked as a priest in the slums of South London, near the Elephant and Castle, in the 1890s. A friend of his, Basil Westcott, who was working in India – the son of the then Bishop of Durham – died of cholera. And Charlie Andrews decided immediately he must go there and take his place.

When, 30 years ago, I visited Andrews' grave in Calcutta, I was much moved by the five words on it. It simply said: *'Deenabandhu*: Friend of the Poor.' It was clear that Andrews had often thought of the poor of Calcutta and Delhi and elsewhere – and said to himself something like *'All you need is Love'*. But in one of his books he put that statement very clearly. He wrote: 'Charity is the careful enquiry into the need of one's fellow men that enables one to give the exact help needed.' That has, of course, much in common with William Blake's: 'He who would do good to another must do it in Minute Particulars.'

William Blake, Charlie Andrews – two men. How about a woman on Love – on 'All you need is Love'?

Whenever I think of the meaning of Love, I find myself thinking of the great English saint: Julian of Norwich. Julian lived nearly 700 years ago. She was what's called an 'anchorite' – a hermit – a recluse. She lived next door to St Julian's church in Norwich – from which she probably took her name.

When she was about 30, she became seriously ill; and it was during her illness – when she was at death's door – that she had a series of vivid and dramatic visions – 'shewings' – revelations – of the Crucifixion of Christ. She was given, she says, 'the mind of the Passion'. Julian recovered from her illness, and then spent 15 to 20 years reflecting on the significance of those revelations.

It needs to be said that Julian was living at a terrible time for Britain. Six years after she was born, what's called 'the Black Death' reached Britain – and a third – and possibly half – the population of England died of that plague within only two years. People died suddenly and horribly. The plague was very contagious, and people couldn't die or be buried with dignity. It was like foot-and-mouth disease for animals – last year. And in fact there was also cattle plague in those years of the Black Death and a series of bad harvests and famine. It was at such a time that Julian had her visions, her revelations of the Love of God – at a time when such a revelation was so desperately needed.

One thing is clear: that although Julian was a hermit, she was not cut off from the sufferings that surrounded her. She was aware that identification with Christ must include identification with those for whom He suffered.

Julian said she prayed for 'an actual bodily sight of our Saviour's bodily pains, and of the compassion of Our Lady, and of all his true lovers' who were living at that time and saw His pains.

And at the very end of her writings, her revelations of the Divine Love and her meditations on them – at the very end she has this remarkable paragraph (I read it to you in the English of that time):

> Wouldst thou witten thy Lord's meaning in this thing? Wit is well. Love was his meaning. Who shewed it thee? Love. What shewed he thee? Love. Wherefore shewed he it? For Love. Hold thee therein and thou shalt witten and know more in the same. But thou shalt never know nor witten therein other thing without end.
>
> Thus was I learned that Love was our Lord's meaning.

All you need is Love. Yes. That's true. But to know what Love is you have to embark on a kind of pilgrimage. We each one of us have to make a journey of discovery. We have to pray as Julian prayed to see and understand the Love Our Lord revealed.

11 'Who do *you* say that I am?': Matthew 16:15, St Mary's, Lewisham, 30 June 2002

One of the greatest gifts of being human is our capacity to make judgements. We have to make judgements at work, in sport, in politics – and so on. And we come here today because we've made a judgement. We call ourselves 'Christians'. We've said of Jesus with St Peter: 'You are the Christ.'

Nowadays, we have to face the fact that the number of people who 'call themselves Christians' in Britain has gone down by over a million in ten years. Anglicans have gone down by half a million.

We're also aware these days that, in Britain, we are a multi-faith and multi-racial community. Though, if we add up all the Hindus, Jews, Muslims, Sikhs and Buddhists in Britain today, they only come to about a million and a half – compared with 25 million Anglicans.

Yet the presence of people of other faiths serves to make us think all the more clearly about our own judgement: why we are what we are; why we've answered the question 'Who do you say that I am?' with the answer that Peter gave: 'You are the Christ.'

Our God-given gift of judgement needs to be used not only to answer that question, but to learn why others, alongside us, believe what they believe. Gone are the days when we could happily fill in a form to say we're 'C of E', and simply leave it at that. We need to know why we believe what we believe, and why we don't believe what others believe – just as sincerely. And there are other reasons why we need to be clear what we believe.

There are, for instance, lots of puzzled people around. Uncompromising disbelievers only amount to one in twenty people. Most men – and, even more, women – believe in God. And probably a half of the people of Britain would call themselves 'religious' people and, for instance, pray from time to time. But they remain outside membership of the Church.

Yet, when, for instance, they're bereaved, they may well say to someone they know who goes to church: 'I wish I could believe like you.' And then we really do need to be able to say why we can say, with Peter: 'Thou are the Christ.'

It would be interesting this morning – were there time – to hear from each one of us here just why we're here: why each one of us here is a Christian – and an Anglican. I always find it very interesting to hear people answering that sort of question – not least, I think, because I'm aware that as a child I went to a Methodist Sunday School – and I owe them a lot. But, strictly speaking, I only became Church of England because our Methodist Church, which was a tin tabernacle!, in Chadwell Heath, part of Dagenham – closed down – 70 years ago!

When I ask people, when I go round, why they go to this particular church – not that – they often say, 'Well, we like the way they do things at St Mary's' – or wherever. And that's, of course, a responsible use of judgement. But it doesn't really avoid the question: 'Who do *you* say that I am?' – because our worship needs to be, in the end, an expression of the 'worth-ship' we give to Christ.

Although, for instance, church buildings are very important, and people have every right to say 'We love St Mary's' – as the hymn says:

> We love the place O God
> Wherein thine honour dwells.

But that place, again, is, in the end, only there because the question 'Who do *you* say that I am?' has been answered in a particular way, by clergy and laity, over the years, and the centuries. All this means that churches today – whatever else they do – must take education and teaching very seriously. Of course, that says something about our church schools, but it says something more about teaching and learning within our congregations.

The question in the Gospel today: 'Who do *you* say that I am?' is not only to St Peter, it's to every one of us. And the answer we come to has to be given to our neighbours; to our children; to those of other faiths; to the puzzled people, who, as I've said, form such a large part of our land.

And my impression – going round churches – is that Church of England people, on the whole, enjoy church-going – no harm in that! But it's rather like belonging to a club. It's not something in which we recognize that one of the main requirements is that we learn – learn how to share what we believe – and why – with others. And so we are all the time challenging the world around to consider what we have to offer in the Christian Church. And that means that communication with the world around becomes for every church and each church an 'A-Star' priority. Each church has to see itself as a centre for the proclamation of what we believe: for passing on what we believe to everyone in the locality. I don't suggest that that is simply a kind of intellectual activity. God forbid!

As once the Canon Missioner of St Albans Diocese, when Robert Runcie was Bishop, I was charged with helping every parish in the diocese to be for ever thinking 'How can we here present Christ to the world around us?' Almost every church is a marvellous advertising site. But every member of every congregation is a potential advertisement – or NOT!

Of course, St Peter didn't give his answer to Christ's question as a kind of intellectual answer to an examination question. He had seen Christ. He had watched him ministering to the people in need. His answer was as one person to another person.

Each person has to be in command of his or her answer to the question: 'Who do *you* say that I am?' But we must also be aware that the world around watches us as it watched Jesus.

But there's something else to be said. What we read in today's Gospel is, of course, a dialogue between Jesus and Peter. Jesus was speaking to – addressing – Peter's need. What we need to be able to tell others is not simply about Jesus. It's about how Jesus speaks to us and ministers to us; to our particular needs now. Which means – of course – that we have to be aware of who we are.

The Gospel probably came alive to me most – in my nearly 50 years of ministry – in a group of ten Christian people who met together each week for ten years in the presence of a priest who was skilled in psychotherapy. We were willing to be honest to ourselves as well as to one another. We had to be. And it was costly.

I suspect that English congregations – to use a phrase my mother loved to use: 'keep themselves to themselves'. They are not always able to speak to one another of what Christ means to them personally, with their particular needs and problems. And our ability to help others is limited by our willingness to go deep in our knowledge of ourselves.

But a last point. In the dialogue in today's Gospel, Jesus was drawing his disciples into close sympathy with himself, before his journey to the Cross, when he put the question of Peter: 'Who do *you* say that I am?' The disciples had so far kept their guesses to themselves, but the time had come for them to declare with confidence the conviction that had been dawning on them: 'You are the Christ – Son of the living God.'

And that declaration was not just something, so to speak, between Jesus and Peter – two earthly friends. It meant that Peter said Jesus was the self-revelation of God – for the healing of him, Peter, and the whole world. And it meant more even than that. Peter saw Jesus as God's revelation of Himself for time and for eternity – for this world and for whatever lies beyond this world.

So the question for us all: 'How do we see Jesus Christ?' is not only about this life and this world – and that's large enough – it's a matter of life and death and takes us even beyond this world.

Which brings us back to where we are now, to this Eucharist this morning here at St Mary's; to this 'act of worship', in which we approach the Father, the Lord, the Friend revealed in Jesus the Son, the Crucified Lord: the Christ.

It is in worship over the years that we come to learn the full meaning of Peter's response: 'You are the Christ' and can be where we learn to make Peter's response our own.

These are testing times for the Church – for Christians – and, not least, for Anglicans. When you make your Communion today, may I suggest that, as you approach the altar, you hear afresh God the Holy Spirit asking you 'Who do *you* say that I am?' and that you make your answer afresh, with new resolution, and commitment:

'You are the Christ, the Son of the living God.'

12 St Mary Magdalene Patronal Festival: St Mary Magdalene, Richmond, 21 July 2002

I count it a very great privilege to be asked to preach at your Patronal Festival today. I almost feel one of your family here, since I've known Julian for over 50 years, since he was about six or seven, and I was a curate to his father, at St Stephen's, Rochester Row in Westminster, where I was ordained, 50 years ago this Michaelmas. I've treasured Julian's friendship over the years and admired the developing pattern of his ministry – from India to Poplar to Chatham to Milton Keynes to Richmond. However, this is not the feast of St Julian of Richmond but of St Mary Magdalene. So let me turn at once to my text; from the Gospel for today – St John's Gospel, Chapter 20, verse 16:

> He saith unto her, 'Mary';
> She turned and saith to him, 'Rabboni' – which is Hebrew
>   for 'Teacher'.

At the heart of a great deal of true religion there is a simple dialogue between the soul and God, and that dialogue is at the heart of most of the great faiths. It's a dialogue that takes many forms. It's often present in the artist and the musician. But for the Christian and the Jew that dialogue is profoundly personal:

> He saith unto her, 'Mary';

> She turned and saith to him, 'Rabboni' – which is Hebrew
> for 'Teacher'.

I begin there today because your Patronal Festival is, not least, the celebration of that dialogue between Mary Magdalene and Jesus: the dialogue of Mary with Jesus, risen from the grave, and at first, difficult to recognize, indeed, Mary mistakes Jesus for the gardener. But, as I've said: I want to suggest your Patronal Festival is also the celebration of the dialogue between the soul and God, which lies at the very heart of much that we know as true religion. There's a great deal of questioning at the moment about the future shape of religion in England – and not only in England. I believe that at such a time, it's right to return to fundamentals: and the first fundamental, I believe, is that dialogue between the soul and God.

> He saith unto her, 'Mary'.

God has called each one of us by our name – at our birth, indeed at our creation. And he waits for us to reply: 'Rabboni' – which is Hebrew for 'Teacher'. Maybe the completion of that dialogue has to wait until – and beyond – our dying day. But I believe it's one of the primary tasks of, for instance, your Team Ministry here in Richmond to foster and feed that dialogue in the name and in the power of Christ. Whenever and wherever that dialogue takes place with integrity, all sorts of other facets of Life Together will be manifest. Worship will be living worship. The Church will be a welcoming church, for it will know that one of its prime responsibilities is to foster that dialogue in everyone who comes near the church. It will be a sustaining church – that cares personally for the congregation and for the parish:

> for those who have articulated their response;
> for those whose response is inarticulate as yet;
> and for those in whom religion is seemingly dead.

It's my experience that, even for many who come to church, the dialogue between their soul and God is relatively inarticulate; and it is for the Church to help and enable that dialogue to become articulate through its various forms of ministry.

> He saith unto her, 'Mary';
> She turned and saith to him, 'Rabboni' – which is Hebrew
> for 'Teacher'.

It may be worth reflecting a little on that dialogue between Jesus and Mary. Mary was drawn to Christ because she experienced through Him the loving power of forgiveness. That made her devoted to Jesus. But the crucifixion had taken Him away from her as a living being and even his corpse had been taken away from the tomb. Mary was desperate to find what she had lost. She was in turmoil and despair like many bereaved people. But she continued to search . . . And her search was rewarded. As it is for many in bereavement. Mary heard Jesus call her name.

> He saith unto her, 'Mary';
> She turned and saith to him, 'Rabboni' – which is Hebrew
> for 'Teacher'.

That's how Mary heard Jesus call. I wonder how you think Jesus calls you? Has called you? Is calling you now? How his call to you has been articulated? And how your response to Him has become – or will become – articulate or more articulate? Perhaps you would allow me to say that this is simply your Sunday celebration – the Sunday celebration of your Patronal Festival. But, as I look around, I can't help wondering what each one of you will be doing on Monday, because what you will be doing on Monday will also be showing just what the call of Christ means to you, in the world. Christ will be calling you at eleven o'clock tomorrow morning as much as he calls you here and now. He doesn't call us and say 'Mary', 'Stephen', 'Robert', 'Helen' – whatever – simply inside a church. Each one of us needs to hear Christ calling wherever

65

we happen to be on Monday – in our home; in our relationship; in our job; in our responsibilities for our locality – and for our world at large – in this post-September 11th world.

I can't in fact preach to you on this subject of the dialogue between the soul and God without saying something about a subject which has had an important history in the life and thought of the Church: the subject of our calling and vocation. It's a very big subject – and a complex one, with a long history – but, as I say, an important one.

Different Christian denominations – Lutheran, Calvinists, Roman Catholic – have given it different emphases. But all would have to agree that the idea of Christ calling to us is very important in the New Testament. That word 'calling' is used again and again by St Paul.

You will probably know that for Roman Catholics, over the centuries, the word 'religious' came to mean simply monks and nuns. But the Second Vatican Council – in the 1960s – made it clear that celibacy, though still a vocation, was not a superior calling to marriage. To be a priest was not superior to being a layman or woman; but each of us needed to take the calling of God seriously.

As I've said: the subject of the calling of God to us is a complex subject. It has something to say about leisure as well as work – and that is where, not least, art and music come in – and sport and relaxing the body. Thank God for Haydn's *Creation* last night at the Proms – and Tiger Woods' golf at Muirfield! Thinking about our calling means thinking about the circumstances and situations which compel some people to do a particular job; but it also means thinking of those for whom there's no alternative but unemployment.

Once upon a time, people called Baker and Miller and Smith, made clear by their very name the job which was theirs for life. But in Richmond, I suspect – from my years as Preacher to Gray's Inn – there are more lawyers per square mile than anywhere else in the land – and maybe the world! And it's important wherever we are – whatever we do – to consider the subject of God's call to us. What God's call should mean, for instance, to a lawyer or an accountant.

It's important in Richmond to ask questions about what the Jewish philosopher, Martin Buber called the I–THOU relationship, which involved not only dialogue between the soul and God – of which I've already spoken this morning – but the relationship to which Buber gave the title of another book of his *Between Man and Man* – about our relating to God through our relations with one another. So I come back again to that marvellous dialogue between Mary Magdalene and Jesus.

> He saith unto her, 'Mary';
> She turned and saith to him, 'Rabboni' – which is Hebrew
>   for 'Teacher'.

I said earlier that this year – in only two months time – I hope to celebrate my fiftieth anniversary of my ordination as a priest. I hope it's clear to you that I have never felt that the word 'vocation' should be applied only to ordained ministry. Yet, when Michaelmas this year arrives, I shall be able to say a heartfelt thanksgiving to God, who I've no doubt called me to be a priest, and gave me a vocation which I have found totally fulfilling – using all such gifts as I have – beginning, as I've said, when Julian, your Rector, was 'no but a lad'!

But today I've not wanted to concentrate on my vocation, or indeed, on vocation to the priesthood. I believe that that dialogue which is at the very heart of today's Gospel should speak to each one of us – speak to us in this world of hungry bodies as well as souls, and bodies afflicted not least by the pandemic of AIDS.

So, as we prepare to receive today the Body of Christ and to come to the altar rail at this Festival Eucharist of St Mary Magdalene – whatever our age, whatever our job, whatever our status in life – let us, each one of us open our hearts again to the voice of God – who has called each one of us into existence and who goes on calling us by name till our very last hours on earth – and beyond.

> He saith unto her, 'Mary';
> She turned and saith to him, 'Rabboni' – which is Hebrew
>   for 'Teacher'.

13 The fiftieth anniversary of my ordination to the priesthood: St Stephen's Rochester Row, 29 September 2002

Two texts. From the Gospel for today, John 1:48, Nathaniel asked him 'Where did you come to know me?' The second, St Luke's Gospel, the second chapter, the thirteenth and fourteenth verses, 'And suddenly, there was with the angels, a multitude of the heavenly host, praising God and saying "Glory to God in the highest and, on earth, peace to all in whom he delights."'

This could be a very long sermon – fifty years long – at least! In fact I simply want to give thanks today for all those who have supported me on my way to ordination, and in the succeeding years.

And my first thanks today must be to Philip, your new vicar, and to the churchwardens, for inviting me to be here with you this morning and to preach to you.

'There was with the angels – *with the angels* – a multitude of the heavenly host.' I'm very aware this morning of those who've supported me over the years but are now 'with the angels'.

I have to say, my mother played a huge part in the beginnings of my vocation to the priesthood by sending me to Sunday School.

My grandfather – my mother's father – was a grocer in Camden Town, and my father's father was a gas-fitter in Camden Town. But he was also for 43 years the organist and choirmaster of the local Presbyterian Church, where my father and mother met.

Just before I, their fourth child, arrived, my mother and father and the three children moved out ten miles east of Bow Bells, to Chadwell Heath, Dagenham – and became Methodists – because there was no Presbyterian Church. So I went to a Methodist Sunday School which I remember only with gratitude and delight.

My favourite hymn there was one which people don't often sing these days, but it had a marvellous tune by Sir Arthur Sullivan, and superb words – about the child Samuel – that still have power to move me. Let me read them to you, because they've meant much to me:

> Hushed was the evening hymn,
> The temple courts were dark,
> The lamp was burning dim
> Before the sacred ark,
> When, suddenly, a voice divine
> Rang through the silence of the shrine.
>
> The old man, meek and mild,
> The priest of Israel, slept;
> His watch the temple child,
> The little Levite, kept:
> And what from Eli's sense was sealed
> The Lord to Hannah's son revealed.
>
> O give me Samuel's ear,
> The open ear, O Lord,
> Alive and quick to hear
> Each whisper of Thy word;
> Like him, to answer at Thy call,
> And to obey Thee first of all.
>
> O give me Samuel's heart,
> A lowly heart, that waits
> Where in Thy house Thou art
> Or watches at Thy gates

By day and night – a heart that still
Moves at the breathing of Thy will.

O give me Samuel's mind,
A sweet unmurmuring faith,
Obedient and resigned
To Thee in life and death,
That I may read with childlike eyes
Truths that are hidden from the wise.

I wonder who remembers that hymn now?

My mother was the youngest of ten children. The next one up – her brother – trained to be a priest (in the Church of England) at a place called Kelham – the Society of the Sacred Mission. And my mother held before me the example of my uncle, who, after his ordination, went out to British Guiana, but was soon taken very ill with malaria and had to settle in Canada, in Ottawa. I only met him once – he could only afford to come back to England once, in the 1930s – by ship, of course. But when he died, he left me his prayer books; and there, in the lists of those he prayed for regularly, was my name.

'There was – with the angels – a multitude of the heavenly host.' And I think gratefully today of my mother, and father, and my uncle, within that heavenly host.

Our Methodist Church at Chadwell Heath closed down. It was a tin tabernacle with a corrugated iron roof. So we moved to the Church of England; and I became, at about six, a choirboy. But today, I have to thank God for that Methodist Church and for all that I've received as a choirboy from Church Music in the Church of England.

As a choirboy, you learn so much from the Bible. And it was as a choirboy that I first heard my text for today, which we sang, then, as part of Handel's *Messiah*: 'And suddenly, there was with the angels a multitude of the heavenly host, praising God and saying, "Glory to God in the highest . . .".'

I started to learn the organ at a very young age. My father's sister was organist of the Presbyterian church at Goodmayes, quite near us, and she taught me. But my mother had first patiently taught me my first notes on the piano. So I thank God today not only for church music but for music – which can give voice to our thankfulness to God and also to all the mysteries of our existence, joyful and sorrowful. Music was my favourite subject at school – and, in fact, was the only subject I was very good at.

The first Sunday of the Second World War – 3 September 1939 – I played for my first service at our church, because the organist, who was a school teacher, had been evacuated that week with his school. I was simply petrified at having to play the organ for a service; but I was even more petrified when, five minutes after the service had started, an Air Raid Warden came in and shouted, 'Take cover! Air raid!'. I got under the organ stool – a fat lot of good that would have done! But, mercifully, the Air Raid 'All clear' sounded quite soon.

My father decided to take me away from school and send me out to work. So, in 1939, as a 14-year-old, I became an office boy in a Norwegian shipping firm in the City. But, seven months later, in April 1940, Germany invaded Norway and that shipping firm immediately closed down. I remember I had to look after a Norwegian ship's captain, Einar Tvedt, whose ship was in London docks but whose wife and family were in Norway. Understandably, he was very anxious and distressed, and my heart went out to him.

Many people were then being called up, so I easily got another job – at a riverside wharf on the north bank of the Thames, close to London Bridge. But, three months later, on the night of 7 September 1940, that wharf on the north bank was one of the many places destroyed by bombs – with huge loss of life in London that night.

On the Monday morning, I made my way to work, clambering over hoses on the ground, and watched that wharf still ablaze. Then I made my way across Southwark Bridge to another wharf we owned, on the site of what is now the Globe Theatre. And there I was to stay working until I left, six years later, to train for ordination, in 1946.

In fact, I think working at that riverside wharf from 1940 to 1946 was virtually the beginning of my training for the ministry. Each day from eight in the morning until five in the evening, I had to deal with orders from drivers of horses and carts lined up outside the wharf and from the barges that were loading and unloading. The men who worked at the wharf all lived near the wharf – in Bermondsey, Rotherhithe and Southwark. Their families were often at night sheltering in the Underground. Their homes were often badly damaged or even destroyed by bombing. I would often have lunch with some of the men in the crane box. The gap between office workers and labouring men virtually disappeared for the duration of the war, as did trades unions.

But I haven't yet told you that in 1939, at the outbreak of the war – and I hardly dare tell you this – I had the nerve to answer an advertisement in the *Musical Times* for a deputy organist at Southwark Cathedral. When the organist, Dr Cook, saw that I was only 14, he said to me, 'I'm sorry, but I'm afraid the choir men won't obey someone who's only fourteen. But I'd like to take you on as a pupil. How much can you afford?' 'Well,' I said, 'I earn fifteen shillings a week, and five shillings goes on fares and five shillings goes to my mother for housekeeping.' 'How would it be if you gave me £5 every three months?' said Dr Cook. So I became the pupil of a marvellous teacher, who, when he'd been sub-organist of Worcester Cathedral, had been close to people like the composer, Sir Edward Elgar. I had lessons in the Cathedral in my lunch hours – until the Cathedral was blitzed, and we had to move to the organ of Guy's Hospital Chapel.

But a kind of dialogue had been set up in my heart and mind: between that riverside wharf and the Cathedral. That dialogue has never ceased – inside me, so to speak – between that marvellous Cathedral with its beauty, and its associations with Shakespeare and Lancelot Andrewes; with its sermons in stone and music – and the riverside: a dialogue, as George MacLeod of Iona used to say, between 'Glory to God in the highest' and 'Glory to God in the High Street'.

Dr Cook is long since dead, and so are people I heard sing in the

Cathedral – like Kathleen Ferrier. And people with whom I worked at the wharf are dead – one as a bomber pilot over Germany. They are part of 'the multitude of the heavenly host' I think of today, enabling me to sing Glory to God in the Highest, and Glory to God in the High Street.

There is one other person I particularly want to mention.

In September 1939 a soldier was billeted on our vicarage in Chadwell Heath: John Rowe. We soon became great friends. He had been studying for ordination with the Community of the Resurrection, Mirfield, but had decided to join up. I possess a birthday and a Christmas present from John from 1939 until he died, as Vicar of a church in Bath, in 1969. He was only 50, but by that time he had been Vice-Principal at Wells Theological College. I was godfather to one of his children who, alas, died tragically young.

On 10 May 1941, I went with John to Queen's Hall, near Broadcasting House, for a performance of Elgar's *Dream of Gerontius*, at half past two on a Saturday afternoon. It was John's twenty-first birthday. I heard the words of 'Praise to the Holiest in the Height', sung, then, in the context of the *Dream of Gerontius*, set to Elgar's music, by the Royal Choral Society. As soon as it was over, John had to go back to his barracks at the Duke of York's Headquarters in Sloane Square. I made my way home. The siren went as soon as I got home, and, that night, Queen's Hall was destroyed, with all the instruments of the orchestra, and much else. There was much loss of life. But the message of the *Dream of Gerontius* that I heard that afternoon was indestructible. I have never forgotten a phrase the Angel sang:

> Learn that the flame of the Everlasting Love doth burn ere it transform.

The message of the Angel was also:

> Praise to the Holiest in the Height
> And in the depths be praise

> In all his works most wonderful
> Most sure in all his ways.

I thank God today for a great company of friends – like John – without whom I may never have been ordained. I thank God for many of them now amongst 'the multitude of the heavenly host'.

One of those friends, Cuthbert Bardsley, became Provost of Southwark Cathedral in 1944, and became my confessor and, later, Bishop of Coventry. He helped me make up my mind about ordination and introduced me to Canon Eric Abbott, who lived at 21, Vincent Square, two minutes from here. He had just become Dean of King's College, London, in the Strand. He became not only my mentor but one of my closest friends; but he also made it clear that ordination would mean, first of all a year at night school – while still at work – learning Latin, New Testament Greek, Geography, Mathematics, Roman History and English. Those were the days! It wasn't easy. I had to begin by gaining confidence that I had a brain at all. You often need others to convince you that you have anything of worth to give. Eric Abbott, above all, did that for me.

It was only after another five years' training that I was ordained deacon in St Paul's Cathedral to a place called St Stephen's Rochester Row! . . . where there was a very notable vicar, George Reindorp, and a very lively congregation. Many of them are now 'with the angels', as are most of the curates who were here when I joined the staff: John Chisholm, David Loake, Hilton Nicholson.

As I said, I won't talk to you this morning about my time here. The point of this sermon is two-fold: it's to ask you to rejoice with me and with the angels, and with the multitude of the heavenly host. For, a year after I was made deacon to come here, I was ordained priest, again on the Feast of St Michael and all Angels; and this morning the words of the Holy Communion – which I first celebrated here – 'Therefore with angels and archangels and with all the company of heaven' – will be particularly poignant for me.

But I've preached this sort of sermon today because I'm aware that I wouldn't have 'made it', so to speak, without all sorts of support – angelic – but also much more down to earth: like my friends here, and in Southwark, and St Albans, and round the country, and, indeed, round the globe.

I don't think there's much separating us all today from the angels and archangels and all the company of heaven, but we're not in heaven yet – God knows! The dialogue between the Highest and the High Street has to go on. And there's one phrase in my second text today which we dare not forget, for so many lives and so much suffering may depend on it.

> Glory to God in the highest and on earth *peace* to all in whom he delights.

It cannot be that tens of thousands should parade on the streets of London to express their heartfelt desire for peace – as they did yesterday – and that we should simply turn deaf ears to them.

It is urgent that, at this time, we couple our Christian worship, Christian thought, and Christian action, for peace and goodwill. Such an occasion as this cannot, and must not end looking backwards – nor can it simply look upwards. There is some ministry still for all of us in God's world, not least striving for peace.

But I was very clear I should preach to you today on those two texts: 'Where did you come to know me?'

'And, suddenly, there was with the angels, a multitude of the heavenly host , praising God and saying, "Glory to God in the highest and, on earth, peace to all in whom he delights." '

14 Remembrance Day: St Mary's Primrose Hill, 10 November 2002

I think I have no need to pretend to you – on Remembrance Day – that my sermon this morning emanated from a particular biblical text. Though there are several I might have taken – like that almost unbearable dialogue between the malefactors, crucified with Jesus, and Jesus Himself: 'Lord, remember me when thou comest into thy Kingdom'; and Jesus' response from his cross: 'Today shalt thou be with me in Paradise.' Or what Matthew tells us happened to Peter, after the crucifixion: 'And Peter remembered the word of Jesus, which said unto him: "Before the cock crow thou shalt deny me thrice." And he went out, and wept bitterly.' Or St Paul's last instruction to Timothy: 'Remember Jesus Christ risen from the dead.' Or, at this Remembrance Day Eucharist, why should we search further than St Luke's Gospel: 'Do this in remembrance of Me'?

But, as I said, I'm not going to pretend – on Remembrance Day – that my sermon started from a text. It did not. It began with my reading recently a new biography – one of the best I've ever read – the biography of Wilfred Owen, now, I suppose, one of the most popular poets of the twentieth century, and one of the greatest of the War Poets. It's by the acknowledged authority on Owen: Dominic Hibberd. His biography of Owen has helped me to prize afresh the great gift – the marvel and mystery of memory – and to revalue remembrance.

Hibberd brings new information and re-interpretation to virtually every aspect of Owen's life – his family background; his education; his struggles with religion and with his sexual orientation; his army training; his experiences on the Western Front in the First World War; his return from the Front as a shell-shock case, and his ensuing time at Craiglockhart War Hospital, Edinburgh, undergoing therapy there at the hands of Dr Arthur Brock; and Owen's development as a poet over the years – not least through his friendship with Siegfried Sassoon, after their providential meeting at Craiglockhart. And, finally, Owen's tragic last year, with his return to the Front in France – and with his death in action, on 4 November 1918 – only a week before the Armistice. The news of his death only arrived at his home on the very day the Armistice was signed.

On Remembrance Day 84 years on, I do not think I need to quote more alongside that tragic fact than the words Owen himself wrote for the Preface of his book of poems, first published in 1920: 'Above all, this book is not concerned with Poetry. The subject of it is War, and the pity of War. The Poetry is in the pity.'

And my sermon today is not about poetry. Nor, in the end, is it about a particular poet. It's about our God-given gift of Memory and Remembrance. And its relevance at such a time as this. No book, as I've said, has ever reminded me more of the marvel and mystery of memory than Hibberd's biography. Each of those aspects of Owen's life, which I've enumerated, speaks to us all of Memory and Remembrance.

When you read in a biography about the childhood of someone like Wilfred Owen, you are almost bound to remember – and compare and contrast it with your own memory – your own childhood surroundings and upbringing. When you read of someone's schooling, again, you remember your own. When you read of someone's first job, you do the same. And so with their struggles with religion, and sexuality. But when you read of Owen's experience on the Western Front, his memories may be similar to many at the time; but our memories, even of, say, the Second World War, are unlike what happened to them. Yet Owen's memories in his poems tell us what we could not otherwise have understood so profoundly. And he tells us:

> All the poet can do today is to warn.
> That is why the true poet must be truthful.

So his remembrance, in, for instance, his *Anthem for Doomed Youth*, makes our remembrance more realistic and profound and searching:

> What passing bells for those who die as cattle?
> Only the monstrous anger of the guns.
> Only the stuttering rifles' rapid rattle
> Can patter out their hasty orisons.

And in his poem *Pro Patria Mori* he wrote:

> If you could hear, at every jolt, the blood
> Come gurgling from the froth-corrupted lungs,
> Bitter as the cud
> Of vile, incurable sores on innocent tongues –
> My friend, you would not tell with such high zest
> To children ardent for some desperate glory
> The old lie: *Dulce et decorum est*
> *Pro patria mori*.

And Owen has a memory that reaches, penetrates to almost mystical levels of understanding: In his poem *Strange Meeting*, he wrote:

> It seemed that out of battle I escaped
> Down some profound dull tunnel, long since scooped
> Through granites which titanic wars had groined . . .

That poem – *Strange Meeting* – describes – as a memory – an unearthly encounter:

> 'Strange friend', I said, 'here is no cause to mourn.'
> 'None', said the other, 'save the undone years,
> The hopelessness . . .'

And in that poem's last lines there is a line of eight words that brings our remembrance to a new level of truth:

I am the enemy you killed, my friend

Owen teaches us today through his memory. He educates our remembrance through his. He warns us through his memory. But after that experience at the Front he was withdrawn, with shell-shock, and a skilled psychotherapist, at Craiglockhart, outside Edinburgh, helped him confront his memories.

No doubt there will be some here today who have known the healing of their memories – indeed, of their selves – through the ministry of a psychotherapist; and their memory will bring understanding and sympathy with Owen. Most of our memories need some healing, and at some depth.

But Craiglockhart was not the end for Owen.

It is we, not Owen, who, in the end, look back at his life and death. But we can thankfully use his words, in his poem *Futility*, as we think today upon all those who gave – and who may yet be called to give – their lives in war. He asks: 'Was it for this the clay grew tall?'

There are two aspects of Hibberd's biography of Owen to which I must particularly draw your attention. The first forms a whole chapter, early on in the biography, a chapter entitled 'Parish Assistant'. When Owen was technically an undergraduate of London University, he took up residence at Dunsden Vicarage, outside Reading, to earn a little money by assisting the evangelical Vicar, Herbert Wigan. Owen was also there to prepare himself for the next stage in his academic progress which meant passing an exam in five subjects: Latin, Roman History, English, French and Botany.

Earlier biographical writings have often suggested Owen went to Dunsden intending to be ordained. Whatever Owen's intentions, his time at Dunsden was the undoing of Owen's Christian faith. And the 20-page chapter headed 'Parish Assistant' is followed by another simply headed 'Apostate'. Wilfred said in a letter to the vicar, at the end of his time at Dunsden, that 'he was a boy when he went to the Vicarage at Dunsden, but by the time he left he was an old man'.

I found it both instructive and challenging to read the account of Owen grappling with the problem of belief while in the employ of an Evangelical parish. Owen, at Dunsden, did he but know it, was wrestling – with great honesty and courage – with the question of a faith that could sustain and support him, with his nature and his temperament, in all that lay ahead of him.

There is a second aspect of Hibberd's biography to which I must also draw your attention. It often has to address the question of Wilfred's younger brother, Harold.

Harold was four years younger than Wilfred, and after the war, would inevitably have much responsibility, on behalf of the family, for Wilfred's letters, papers and poems. But – to put the matter simply – Harold was an unreliable editor: destroying some of Wilfred's manuscripts; omitting what embarrassed him and thanking Sassoon for burning several of Wilfred's outspoken and revealing letters. Harold would have loved Wilfred to have been a devout Christian with no sexual ambiguity. Here again is the question of honesty and remembrance.

You will understand now, I hope, why I have thought it appropriate to centre my sermon today on Hibberd's biography. For it does more than take us back to Owen and to 1918. It challenges us now to be as honest as we can with our memories and our remembrance. 'Was it for this the clay grew tall?' suddenly becomes a question about ourselves – and about the lives that surround us now – in England and Iraq and Palestine and Israel and the United States . . . and Russia. And we come here to this Remembrance Day Eucharist because it is not enough simply to let our memories go back to 1918 or 1945 or to the Falklands – to 11 September or to Bali or Moscow.

We come here to this Eucharist for our memories – and not only our memories – to be healed. We come here for our vision and hope and resolution, indeed, for ourselves to be made new.

And we do this in 'remembrance'. We bring to the altar today

Wilfred Owen and all who died as cattle – who die as cattle – and who may yet die as cattle. And we pray 'Lord remember them' – and us – in our present dilemmas and with our present faith and lack of it. We pray for God to purge our memories, our understanding and our wills.

Wilfred Owen has, of course, spoken powerfully to many over the years, not least to Benjamin Britten. He speaks powerfully this year through the exhibition at the Imperial War Museum: 'Anthem for Doomed Youth'. We pray today that he will speak to us. And we ask that the warning of the poet may speak to us in our remembrance and make us listen. And may our remembering and our recalling above all help us to face our true selves and remind us why our clay has been allowed to 'grow tall'.

15 The installation of Anthony Hawley as Canon Residentiary of Liverpool: Liverpool Cathedral, 30 November 2002

John 6:9: Andrew said: 'There is a lad here with five barley loaves and two small fish; but what are they amongst so many?'

Sometimes when I'm asked to preach, I find that a text, or even just a phrase, comes to me almost as a command. It was so with those five words: 'There is a lad here.' As soon as Anthony told me he was to be made a Canon Residentiary of this great Cathedral, and did me the huge honour of inviting me to preach at his installation today – the Feast of St Andrew – I knew I must preach to you on those words from St John's Gospel: 'Andrew said: "There is a lad here . . ."' But then I had to begin to think what I should say!

Maybe it was a kind of 'Liverpool Echo' in my heart and mind – from those famous four Liverpool 'lads', who, in the Sixties, 'shook the world'!

My friendship with Anthony began over 30 years ago, when he was Director of the Charterhouse-in-Southwark Settlement, and priest-in-charge of St Hugh's, the Charterhouse Mission in Southwark. It was, and is, one of the best inner-city projects in all South London, not least where the Youth Work was concerned. Many a schoolboy came up from the country, from Charterhouse – the public school at Godalming – to learn about Southwark's inner-city problems, and to take part in the youth work of the Settlement.

'There is a lad here . . . but what is that amongst so many?' takes me straight back to that densely populated area of South London, ten minutes or so from London Bridge, where I also had lived, round the corner, when I was canon of Southwark, in the Sixties.

'There is a lad here . . .' You will forgive me, now 77 years of age, if I say that, when I think back to the days of Anthony at the Charterhouse Mission, when he was 'no but a lad', I think 'there was a lad there' – and there was a lass: Rosemary.

But now let me take you on a dozen and more years – to 1984.

I had succeeded in persuading my good friend of many years, a Liverpudlian named Robert Runcie, to set up his Commission on Urban Priority Areas that produced the Report *Faith in the City*. The Commission decided to begin its work by undertaking a series of visits to particular areas in our major cities. The very first visit was unforgettable. It was to Liverpool. During the day – the first day of that visit – I was taken to Kirkby to see Centre 63 at work, and hear what it did. It was not unlike the Charterhouse Mission.

That evening, we held our first public meeting as a Commission in Centre 63 itself with the then Bishop of Liverpool, David Sheppard, in the Chair. In the break for tea, in the middle of the meeting, I shall never forget talking with a man who had been employed by Tate and Lyle, but was one of the many by then unemployed. He was the very picture of dejection – and rejection.

That weekend I visited Cantril Farm, Skelmersdale and Toxteth. The then Vicar took us round Kirkby, and we came on here, to the Cathedral. The problems of Liverpool and Liverpool Diocese seemed to us immense – and were. I think each one of the Commission felt like a lad with only 'five barley loaves and two small fish'. But on that Commission we were given what we asked of God: faith, hope and vision. We were given faith in the City, and a message not simply for the Church of England but for Britain.

You'll understand, I think, with what joy I heard the news, later in

1984, that Anthony – who I knew understood from within Faith in the City – was to be the new team Rector of Kirkby, in a great succession of parish priests there. Anthony and I have been close friends all these years between, and my admiration for his long and faithful ministry at Kirkby – from 1984 until now – knows no bounds.

But let me now take you forward again: to 1988.

It was on Maundy Thursday that I last preached here in this cathedral, at the Eucharist for the Renewal of Vows. I found it a most moving service. I was seated in a stall from where I could observe the communicants, most of them the clergy of the diocese. I don't usually look at people as they come up to receive communion, but that Maundy Thursday I wanted to see each individual who came to the communion rail, and pray for them in their particular vocation and ministry.

'There is a lad here . . .,' I thought. And there's another . . . . And another . . . . A long line of communicants. And each of them a lad – and sometimes a lass – with 'five loaves and two fishes'. But what was that among the densely populated parishes of the diocese with all their problems? The next day, Good Friday, I conducted the Three Hours at Walton – your suffragan bishop, Michael Henshall, and his wife, were, I remember, in the congregation. That, too, was another hugely privileged occasion for me.

But now I ask you to share a very different experience. Six years later, Anthony helped me in a most marvellous way.

Bishop Trevor Huddleston had asked me to write his biography. By way of preparation I did several journeys following in his footsteps. In 1994 I planned to travel to where he had been Archbishop of the Indian Ocean – more than a dozen years before.

Anthony, with great generosity, agreed to accompany me – to the Seychelles; to Madagascar, and to Mauritius. It was particularly kind of Rosemary to let me 'borrow her husband' – to use the wonderful phrase of Graham Greene. And, after Anthony had conducted the morning service at Kirkby, he and Rosemary drove all the way to Gatwick. And soon, Anthony and I were learning together about the 70,000 people of the Seychelles.

We stayed with the Bishop and his wife and family. Then we went on to Madagascar – with its 12 million people, and its huge problems – with half the people under 15 years of age. I remember the Bishop's car breaking down, and Anthony and the Bishop's daughter changing the wheel, under a blazing sun – while the Bishop and I looked on – admiringly!! For much of the time in Madagascar Anthony and I stayed with a wonderful Christian family – with whom we're still in contact – Prosper and Chantal Razafinarivo.

From Madagascar we went on to Mauritius – another million people – half of them Hindus and Muslims. We came to the Province of the Indian Ocean with our 'five loaves and two small fishes'.

Needless to say, those weeks together greatly strengthened our mutual friendship, so that whenever I thought and prayed for Anthony in Kirkby and for the church here it was the prayers and thoughts of a friend for a friend. And again, you'll understand, it was with great joy that I heard, earlier this year, that the Bishop had appointed Anthony – with all his gathered experience – to be a Residentiary Canon here. I read Anthony's job specification as a Canon here with what I will call affectionate and enthusiastic interest:

> He should be ready to attend meetings of deanery synods and chapters, and, in particular, to foster good working relationships with the deaneries of Liverpool North and Toxteth and Wavertree. He shall endeavour to strengthen the whole corporate life, worship and work of the Cathedral, and to promote the use of the Cathedral in the Diocese. He shall have a particular concern for the ministry of the Cathedral to visitors, whether they be tourists, pilgrims, church parties, or people in need of help.

And now, from today, 'There is a lad here – with five barley loaves and two small fish.'

When a preacher starts thinking about a sermon, he usually first explores the setting of his text in the Gospel, and at the beginning of the sermon expounds its setting there, and then moves out to the world. I decided today I wanted to end my address to you by thinking more about the setting of my text in the gospel. But I wanted to do that in a particular way. Let me explain.

Over fifty years ago, when I was still a student at King's College, London, the Dean of the College, Eric Abbott, who became my closest friend as well as my mentor, read a poem to us one evening in chapel. I have never forgotten it and I have read that poem each year since I was ordained. It's by a Roman Catholic, Caryll Houselander. She lived within the parish to which I was ordained, in Westminster – not far from Westminster Cathedral. She was often to be seen walking about Westminster and going into the Cathedral to pray.

That poem – which she called *Philip Speaks* – has meant as much to me in my life as any other poem. And I had no hesitation in deciding to read it to you today to bring to an end, and, so to speak, to sum up, my sermon for Anthony's installation.

> When we returned and told Him all we had done,
> I for one was emptied out like a husk
> that has scattered its seed upon hard ground.
>
> We had not had time even to eat;
> always the open hand,
> always the blind eyes,
> always the deaf ears,
> always the wounds to be healed.
>
> My thoughts were like wild birds
> beating the bars of the cage
> for empty skies.
>
> Even now the smell of the people
> clung to my hair and clothes,
> a rotten sweetness of oil and musk
> that smells like death, it hung in my hair.
>
> Their voices went on and on in my head,

monotonous waves wearing my mind away; -
rock is worn by the waves to sand.
I wanted to shut my mind that my thoughts might close
on my own peace, I wanted to close
the peace of my love in my heart
like dew in a dark rose.

He told us to rest.

We went in a small ship,
the wind and water moving in her,
She lived in their sweetness of life, a bride.
Her sail a white wing, unmoving, moved with the tide.
She lay to the wind, and we gave our hearts with a sigh
to the breath of the spirit of love.

But when we came to the shore
the people were there;
they had found us out.
Always the open hand,
always the blind eyes,
always the deaf ears,
always the wounds to be healed!
They were there,
swarming there, everywhere,
insects there in the sun
when someone has lifted a stone.
I knew they would drain Him
and wring Him out – wring Him out
to the last drop of the fountain water of Life.

I was sick of it all
with a dry husk for a heart
But He saw the flocks wanting shepherd and fold,
pity in Him rose in a clear spring
for the world's thirst, and love was a pastureland.

So it went on all day.
Always the open hand,
always the dull mind,
always the slow heart
always the nameless fears,
and self-pity, self-pity and tears.

Until the sun went up in the blaze of the day's heat
and with red wine burning through thin gold
it was lowered slowly on to the altar stone
of the darkening world, where the sheep were in fold.

We thought 'Now it is night, He will send them away,
The hour is late,' we said, 'this is a desert place,
send them away, Lord, to buy food and be fed!'
But He 'You give them to eat!'

The grass in that place shone exceedingly green,
I remember, because when the brain is dust,
the cool greenness of grass is absurdly sweet.

'There is a lad here,' said Andrew,
'with two little fish and five loaves of bread,
but what are these, if this crowd must be fed?'
'Bid them sit down on the grass and give them to eat,'
the Lord said.

The lad was one of the crowd, he went as he came.
As long as the world lasts, the world will remember him,
but no one will know his name!

They sat down on the grass.
My heart contracted, my mind was withered up,
but Christ poured out His tenderness,
like wine poured out into a lifted cup.

Always the open hands,

always the blind eyes,
always the mouth to be fed,
and I for one was emptied out like a husk
that has scattered its seed upon hard ground.
But He saw the flocks wanting shepherd and fold;
Pity in Him rose in a clear spring
for the world's thirst, and love was a pastureland.

The Lord blessed the bread.
He put it into our hands
and it multiplied,
not in *His* hands but in *mine!*

Even now, remembering this,
my thoughts shut like a folding wing,
my mind is a blank sheet of light
in the mystery of the thing.

I gave and my hands were full, again and again;
Pity in Him fell on my dry dust,
it was summer rain,
and the husk of my heart expanded and filled again,
and was large with grain.

For me, the miracle was this,
that a clear stream of the Lord's love
(not mine)
flowed out of my soul,
a shining wave, over my fellow men.

These things I have told you happened a long while since.
Our cherished Lord is dead, He was crucified.
Now, as then, we go about in the crowd telling His love,
and how He rose from the dead, and risen in us
He lives in the least of men.
But I think nobody understands,

until I touch their wounds and they know
the healing of His hands.

On the night of the Pasch, before He died,
He blessed the bread and put it into my hands,
to increase and be multiplied to the end of time.

Now if I turned my face away from the market place,
I should be haunted,
hearing the rustle of wheat in the darkness,
striving, pushing up to the light.
I should hear His words falling like slow tears
in the Supper room, -
when He prayed that we all be one,
even as we are one, the Father and Son, -
falling like slow tears
over the sown fields,
and I should see the world
like a young field of wheat
growing up for the grain
watered by Christ's tears.

Always the open hands,
always the blind eyes,
always the slow mind,
always the deaf ears,
and always Christ, our Lord,
crowned with the flowering thorn
and ringed with spears.

I know – now that I never see
the print of His feet in the dust
where the Son of Man trod –
that in every man for ever
I meet the Son of God.

16 Gallipoli Memorial Service: Holy Trinity, Eltham, 13 April 2003

Since last November, when I was honoured to receive this invitation to preach this Gallipoli Memorial sermon, it seems to me, and I've little doubt to you, the world has changed. Now I'm preaching about a war that happened nearly 90 years ago – during another war. Yet, when I came to draft my sermon, rightly or wrongly, I did not find that fact greatly altered what I had to say. If what I have to say is worth saying, it will be as true and relevant now as it was last November.

I've chosen a text which calls for each one of us to be recognized and to recognize ourselves as 'stewards of the mysteries of God'. St Paul's First Epistle to the Corinthians: Chapter 4, Verse 1: 'We are to be regarded as ministers of Christ and stewards of the mysteries of God.'

There are, of course, several huge mysteries to this life which are inescapable; and, at this particular service and at this particular time, there are four great mysteries – at least – which I believe we must confront.

First:	The mystery of Time
Second:	The mystery of Place
Third:	The mystery of Persons
Fourth:	The mystery of Good and Evil.

Of course, we shall only be able to glance at these great mysteries this evening; yet I think it's of the utmost importance that we do at least recognize them, and recognize that we are ourselves, by our very existence, stewards of these mysteries of God.

Time – Place – Persons – Good and Evil.

First: Time.

In 1972, I went on a six-month journey between jobs, beginning on New Year's Eve. I went to Nigeria, Ghana, Uganda, Zambia, South Africa, Australia, New Zealand, Fiji, Vanuatu, the Solomon Islands, New Guinea, then back to Australia, Singapore, Hong Kong, India, Sri Lanka, and home.

It was on 25 April 1972, back in Australia, that I wrote in my diary:

> As it was St Mark's Day, I celebrated the Holy Communion at 8 am at St James's Church, in the centre of Sydney. In the vestry was a picture of David Sheppard, in 1956, signing autographs for Islington schoolboys, after leading the England cricketers to victory.
>
> Already, Sydney was alive with be-medalled ex-servicemen getting ready for the ANZAC parade. At 10 am, I went into the city again, to see something of the parade, in which 20,000 soldiers and ex-servicemen were involved. It is incredible how all this has survived in Australia and New Zealand, whereas in England, the day almost goes by unnoticed. I suppose we have other occasions and other ways of celebrating our national identity. As I looked at people in the park in Sydney, the crowds and ex-servicemen, I found myself greatly enjoying their company. It was a celebration and an occasion for pageantry. The parks were packed with people chatting together in the sun, enjoying old times. There were bowler-hatted ex-officers, little ordinary men and big ordinary men. There were bands and pith helmets, scarlet uniforms, bagpipes and kilts; but above all there was the feeling of solidarity born of a great and mutual experience. I don't think that experience should ever be under-rated or despised.

That particular day reminded me, and reminds me now, of the mystery of Time – 25 April 1972 – ANZAC Day – was clearly a great day: not least because it reminded so many of other great days, in 1915, at Gallipoli.

Since 1972, I've read a score of books on Gallipoli: some of them history books; some of them biographies. One of them by a great friend of mine, Geoffrey Moorhouse, looking back on how Gallipoli affected the Lancashire town of Bury, because its local regiment was so tragically involved.

Biography is, of course, a form of history; and history spells out the meaning of time. And Time is the very raw material of our existence: of the existence of each one of us. When you look up in a dictionary the meaning of that four-letter-word 'Time', it may have a whole column, or two, by way of definition. Then you will be left with the mystery of it all: the mystery of it as a kind of stage on which we each one of us strut for a limited time – till the curtain comes down – as it did for so many, at Gallipoli, in 1915. And each of us human beings have to steward that mystery of time – for a time.

It's not without significance that, in the last weeks, our armies have been trampling the ground between the Tigris and the Euphrates, with no time to think of the great civilizations that flourished by those mighty rivers 'once upon a time' – as we say.

First, the mystery of Time. Secondly, the mystery of Place.

I've already mentioned 17 or so particular places – Sydney, Gallipoli, Bury, and so on. But there are others – the Dardanelles – and Suvla Bay. No one who served in Gallipoli was ever likely to forget the place – if he lived to remember.

Place is also a 'stage' – as well as time – a mysterious stage on which we strut. Just think for a second of the places which have formed an inseparable part of your existence: without which your life would be a different life. (In passing, let me say: Who would have thought of Basra and Baghdad as significant places in our lives till a few days ago?)

That ANZAC Day in 1972, when I arrived in Sydney, I had no idea Sydney would enable me to encounter aspects of Gallipoli I'd never encountered before. Before 1972, Gallipoli was for me simply one more date and one more place in Great War history. From 1972 it was significant for me both in the mystery of time and the mystery of place.

Time – Place – and Persons. The mystery of persons.

There are two persons I want to mention before I go any further. I want to mention the vicar of this church, Dr Michael Harrison, without whose kindness I should not be speaking to you this evening. He is one of my closest friends, and every time we meet he helps me to encounter something more of the mystery of existence.

And I want to mention last year's Gallipoli preacher – Andrew Wilson – a vicar in Poplar, and another close friend – who last year preached as moving a sermon as I've ever heard, about his grandfather who was a chaplain at Gallipoli.

Many will be here tonight because they had a relative at Gallipoli. David Machin – another close friend – is here because his father was at Gallipoli – on the battleship HMS *Prince of Wales*. And he has written a memorable paper 'Gallipoli: A Son's Reflections', which will be treasured by his children and his children's children.

But there's one person whom this year and this evening I particularly want to remember. I only met him once – in Bishop's House, Southwark – when Mervyn Stockwood was Bishop: Major – as he liked to be called – C. R. Attlee: Prime Minister, 1945–51. People often mention Winston Churchill when they talk of Gallipoli. Few mention Attlee. Indeed, people tend to underestimate Attlee – even belittle him (Churchill said Attlee was 'a modest little man with much to be modest about'). But on Gallipoli and on the mystery of persons I think Attlee has as much to say to us as Churchill. And Attlee was there.

Clement Richard Attlee had been a public schoolboy at Haileybury – and hated it. In October 1905, a year after leaving Oxford and beginning life at the Bar, an event occurred which Attlee confessed altered the whole course of his life. One evening he paid a visit to the Haileybury Club in Stepney. The East End Boys Club's objects were social and educational. In essence, it did for poor boys what the OTC did for rich boys at public schools. The Club was open five nights a week. And Attlee ran the Cadets at the Club. Wearing uniform, he said, gave the Cadets – all East End lads – a pride which they had never previously enjoyed. The discipline of the Cadets braced them. The team work gave them a sense of belonging.

Though Attlee had been called to the Bar in 1907, he gave up his training as a barrister, left home for good, and for seven years lived at the Haileybury Club in Stepney and managed it, and gave all his next years to the East End. From the Haileybury Club he went on to become Secretary of Toynbee Hall, and, later, became Mayor of Limehouse. But in September 1914, after the outbreak of the war, Attlee was gazetted as Lieutenant to the 6th Battalion of the South Lancashire Regiment – mostly raw lads – just like his Stepney Club lads – but from Wigan, Warrington and Liverpool. Attlee was given command of a company of seven officers and 850 men. The following June – 1915 – the South Lancs sailed from Avonmouth for Gallipoli. (Again, one can't help thinking of those who so recently have been similarly suddenly transported to Iraq.)

When Attlee and the 6th South Lancashires arrived at Gallipoli, they found the British and Australian infantry pinned down in trenches. After a month experiencing the heat, the smells and the flies, like many others, Attlee got dysentery, and was carried off unconscious, so missing the big attack at Anzac where six or seven thousand casualties were inflicted on his Division. Attlee maintained that it was dysentery which had probably saved his life. (Dysentery was the 'providential accident' which probably preserved Attlee to be Prime Minister of England. 'Providential Accidents' are part of the mystery of each person – of each of our lives . . . . 'Some enchanted evening, you may see a stranger across a crowded room' . . . and that moment changes your whole life.) Attlee was shipped off to Hamrun Hospital, Malta, but it wasn't many weeks before he was back with his men at Gallipoli.

Many people vilified Churchill for his part in initiating the Gallipoli Campaign. Paradoxically, Attlee only had praise for him, and believed that the strategy Churchill had conceived came near to a great success which might have shortened the war and saved thousands of lives.

While we are considering the mystery of persons, there is one other person who deserves our attention this evening: the Revd Henry Hall, vicar of this church and parish for 35 years, from 1907 to 1942. He was appointed a Chaplain to the British Army's 29th Division, and was with them when they landed on the West Beach at Gallipoli. We would not be here this evening had not Henry Hall's experience at Gallipoli greatly affected him, and made him set up the Gallipoli Chapel here, in remembrance of those with whom he had served; so many of whom never came home.

There was a fourth mystery that I listed among the mysteries that we must all steward as human beings: the mystery of Good and Evil.

It doesn't surprise me, but it does dismay me, that many of the books I've read on Gallipoli are at a loss to describe what in fact it was all about! Of course, they say it was 'to relieve the pressure on the Western Front'. And of course they say that we were at war with the Turks, and so were the Russians. Britain, France and Russia were lined up against the Austro-Hungarian Empire. Lesser powers – Greece, Italy, Bulgaria – were trying to spot the likely winner before committing themselves. Turkey didn't need to auction herself, so to speak. She could have remained neutral. So what was it all about? What were those 400,000 casualties in eight and a half months all about?

The Australian journalist L. A. Carlyon, in his recent book on Gallipoli, calls one of his chapters 'All for nothing' – and there's no question mark. But he begins the last chapter of his much praised book:

> Gallipoli, the war that got away from its handlers . . . [And there's a warning for us today!] Gallipoli is a tale of all that is fine and all that is foolish in the human condition. If it made more sense, it would be a lesser story. The tale is mostly about frailty. This, along with the beauty of its setting, helps explain why it lingers in the imagination after larger and more important wars are forgotten.

Well, did any good thing come out of Gallipoli? The poet Keats wrote of 'Negative Capability, when a man is capable of being in uncertainties, mysteries, doubts, without any irritable reaching after fact and reason.'

We've already spoken of Clement Attlee. I wonder how much of his greatness as a Prime Minister was related to his experience at Gallipoli. Quite a lot I believe.

Gallipoli wasn't all evil.

Kemal Atatürk was promoted general after Gallipoli. In fact, Kemal only became Atatürk – meaning 'father of the Turks' – after Gallipoli. Turkey became a republic after Gallipoli. The Islamic form of Government ended – under Atatürk.

Often Gallipoli is referred to as the 'blooding' of Australia and New Zealand – a word which suggests some considerable gain – at some considerable – and tragic – cost.

I have left to the end of what I want to say this evening any reference to the fact that we meet – by accident, or design, or Providence – or a mixture of all three – on Palm Sunday evening: the beginning of another Holy Week, which will end, of course, with Good Friday and Easter Day. But I would not be a 'minister of Christ and a steward of the mysteries of God' if I did not believe that the events of the first Holy Week had something literally crucial to say about each of those four huge mysteries that have occupied our thinking this evening.

The mystery of Time.

Even the year of Gallipoli is numbered – 1915 – after the birth of Him whose crucifixion we shall commemorate again on Friday this week. And – as T. S. Eliot reminded us – 'we call this Friday good' – in spite of and, paradoxically, because of all the Evil that happened on it.

This week we shall have the opportunity to think again of the meaning of those events of that first Holy Week and what they say about those who lost their lives at Gallipoli and what they say to us as we confront our world today – riven by war.

The mystery of Place.

I believe the mystery of every place on earth becomes more profound once we have begun to comprehend what God did in Jesus on this earth the first Holy Week – at a particular place – Calvary – in a particular city – Jerusalem.

The mystery of Persons.

Only when we have followed Jesus as He enters Jerusalem; only when we have been with Him in the Upper Room; only when we have watched with him in Gethsemane; only when we have stood by Him on Calvary and heard His words from the Cross:

> Father forgive them, for they know not what they do
> Today thou shalt be with me in Paradise
> Woman, behold thy Son: Son, behold thy Mother
> My God, my God, why hast thou forsaken me
> I thirst
> It is finished. Father, into thy hands I commend my Spirit.

Only when we have spent much time with Jesus crucified, do we begin to understand what God means a person to be in this world, when he brings them to birth, and sustains them, until their time has come to leave this world and return to the Father, as did Jesus himself.

The mystery of Good and Evil.

Again, it's only when we watch that titanic struggle on Calvary that we begin to understand the full meaning of Good and Evil.

In the midst of the 600-page book on Gallipoli that I've already mentioned – by the Australian journalist L. A. Carlyon – there is an extraordinary photograph of a huge mound of human bones – half of them skulls. All of them are the remains of Turkish soldiers. The Turks put their casualties at 251,309 – more than a quarter of a million – including 86,692 dead. Allied casualties were more than 140,000 – Britain lost 21,235 dead; France 10,000; Australia 8,709; New Zealand 2,701.

It was the sight of that dramatic but appalling mound of skulls – each a human life – with a home and family and bereaved loved ones – that gripped me more than the rest of the pages of Carlyon's great book on Gallipoli: a mound of Turkish skulls swept up in 1919.

But as I thought upon that sight, a verse from the Gospels entered my mind and heart. In Matthew, Mark, Luke and John it says that 'when they came to a place called Golgotha – the place of a skull – there they crucified him'.

The mystery of good and evil – and the mystery of the triumphant love of God – was never more clearly expressed and exposed than at Golgotha when they crucified Jesus at the place of a skull. There pure goodness was revealed – and naked evil.

And this very week, Holy Week, we each of us have opportunity – God-given opportunity – not least in thankfulness for the lives laid down at Gallipoli, to think again about the mystery of good and evil and its redemption through the triumphant love of God revealed in Jesus.

God of love, you created each one of us as stewards of your mysteries: of time and place and persons and good and evil. Your redeeming love was embodied in your son Jesus. We commend to your love all those who served at Gallipoli and all who are serving now in Iraq – British, American, Iraqi. And may the power of your unconquerable redeeming Love lighten upon the wastes of the wraths and sorrows of our world today. Amen.

17 The funeral of the Revd Frank Seymour ('Bill') Skelton: Southwark Cathedral, 5 June 2003

It is a very great privilege for me to do what *Chris* has asked me to do: to preach at my good friend Bill's funeral.

Bill and I were friends for nearly fifty years.

I've chosen what may seem to some a somewhat curious text. The Gospel according to St Mark: Chapter 5: Verse 9: 'And he asked him: What is thy name? And he answered, saying, My name is Legion, for we are many.'

The identity of us all is, of course, complex; and we spend much of our lives getting to know who we are, but I think I'm right to say, at the outset, that Bill's identity was of a particular complexity.

To begin at the beginning – *his* beginning. Almost all of us will have known Bill as 'Bill'; but he was born Frank *Seymour* Skelton. And his second name – 'Seymour' – had a special significance. He was the nephew and godson of the Duke of Somerset, who was a Seymour – and carried the sceptre with the cross in procession at the Coronation of 1937; and, at the Duke's invitation, Bill – that memorable day – carried the Duke's coronet, and acted as his page.

Bill was then 16 years of age.

On the rare occasions that Bill talked about his connections with that historic family, and of that great day, he would almost invariably recount how embarrassed he was to travel up from his home at Pirbright to the Abbey, in his page's livery, by public transport. At least part of him that day would undoubtedly have preferred to be plain 'Bill' rather than a Seymour – much as he was proud to be his uncle's page.

Bill's father was a nurseryman and garden designer of distinction; and to the end of his days, Bill loved gardens and gardening.

He was sent away to school at Blundell's, at Tiverton, Devon, through, probably, the generosity of his uncle. Bill didn't much enjoy his schooling. But there was one 'providential accident'. The Blundell's School Missioner was Mervyn Stockwood – later, of course, Bishop of Southwark; and John Robinson – later Dean of Clare and Trinity and Bishop of Woolwich – was the Assistant Missioner. And Mervyn's slum parish of St Matthew's Moorfields, Bristol, received visits from groups of Blundell's schoolboys, of whom Bill was one. And for Mervyn, Bill Skelton, the schoolboy, once seen, was never forgotten. And maybe, it was St Matthew's Moorfields that gave Bill his first thoughts of being a parish priest.

Bill's father died when Bill was only 15, and he therefore left Blundell's to serve an apprenticeship in the City as an accountant. But those years also had something of 'providential accident' about them. Bill's becoming, many years later, Master of the Coopers' Company had its beginnings in those years he spent in the City. Bill was apprenticed in the City to Mr T. G. Rawlins, who himself, in due course, would be Master of the Coopers, and would introduce Bill to them.

For anyone born – like Bill – in 1920, the outbreak of the war, in 1939, meant, of course, National Service; and, in 1940, Bill began a new life in the Royal Air Force.

One thing is certain: no one at Pirbright, no one at Blundell's, no one at the accountants where he was apprenticed, no one – not even the Duke of Somerset – and certainly not Bill himself – had any idea what demands would soon be made on him or the deeds of which he would be capable which would be gathered in those two rare and remarkable decorations: DFC and Bar 44 and DSO and Bar 45.

But there is one book – *Night Fighter* by C. F. Rawnsley and Robert Wright, both of them night fighters, from which today I feel bound to quote a considerable passage:

Of all the crews I knew during the war, the most interesting to my mind, was made up of Branse Burbridge and Bill Skelton. At the end, Branse was one of the Flight Commanders of 85 Squadron, and Bill Skelton was the Navigator or Leader.

Not only were these two the most interesting and capable young men, but they also flew what was probably the most extraordinary of all the long-range escort patrols ever accomplished. Many times I talked over the details of that patrol with other people who belonged to the night fighter world, and we all agreed that it was an outstanding effort. They even had an engine catch fire over Hamburg...

From the moment they crewed up together for their second tour of flying, Branse and Bill hit it off together, both on the ground and in the air. They had the perfect and all too rare understanding that characterised the best crews, and which enabled them to work together almost as one man.

It was not only that Branse was an excellent pilot, and that Bill was a first-rate navigator: they had also developed the ability to anticipate each other's moves, to work with a minimum of chatter and without friction and argument, and almost to read one another's thoughts; and the months of the gruelling work flying from West Malling against the fighter-bombers in the raids on London had put the final polish on their individual skill and on their work as a team. In the far more exacting conditions of offensive operations, where only the master craftsman could hope for consistent success, they climbed the individual scoreboard in a meteoric fashion, and established a record night bag for any one crew of twenty enemy aircraft destroyed.

I think today it is important for us to recognize that we are here only because of the bravery of Bill and Branse Burbridge, and people like them.

When the war was over, Bill rarely spoke of his part in it. Perhaps it was the burden he bore of bereavement of so many of those who flew with him – some of the 55,573 who did not return.

It is surely significant that John Pudney, the poet, who himself served in the RAF during the war, wrote a poem he called *Missing* that began simply with four words:

Less said the better

Bill knew that it was not least by, again, a 'providential accident' – or a series of them – that he was allowed another life. He was still only 25, and knew he must now get on with the next life – in *this* world.

And it was only because he was an ex-serviceman that, with many another ex-serviceman, he went up to Cambridge, to Trinity Hall, where Launcelot Fleming, the Dean and Chaplain, was waiting to welcome him. Branse Burbridge, his RAF crew partner, was a man of strong Christian faith and became a lay preacher. It is likely that Bill's decision to train for ordination was, in part, the product of their partnership. Bill gave himself to his studies; but he also gave himself to rowing, and would be in the Trinity Hall boat that was Head of the River, and rowed at Henley; and, indeed, became one of the best coaches on the river; and wore his Leander scarf with pride.

Bill went from Trinity Hall to Ridley Hall, and, at the end of his time there, was directed to go to the parish of Ormskirk, Liverpool. He was made deacon by Clifford Martin, Bishop of Liverpool in 1950, and ordained priest in 1951. He was disappointed at the training he received in Ormskirk, but several parishioners gratefully remembered Bill long after he left there.

It was in 1952 that John Robinson, then Dean of Clare, and Professor Charlie Moule, who had both remembered Bill, invited him to come back to Cambridge to Clare, as Chaplain, and to have a special responsibility for the Cambridge Pastorate, based on Holy Trinity Church.

When I went up to Cambridge as Chaplain of Trinity, in 1955, I soon set eyes on Bill, and realized what a powerful pastoral ministry he was exercising. Many members of Clare kept in touch with Bill all their lives. He remained one of their closest friends. And the pastorate put him in touch, not least with members of Girton and Newnham. The handsome Bill's Cambridge years – from 1952 to 1959 – were undoubtedly years of unique ministry.

In 1955, Mervyn Stockwood had returned to Cambridge as Vicar of Great St Mary's but in 1959 he was appointed Bishop of Southwark. He asked John Robinson to be Bishop of Woolwich, Bill to be Rector of St Mary's, Bermondsey, and me to be Vicar of St George's, Camberwell – which was the Trinity College Mission. Bill and I were soon seeing a lot of each other in the clergy group which John Robinson set up in Southwark.

Bill was a notable Rector at Bermondsey, not least for his training of clergy and for moulding both clergy and laity into a team. He demanded high standards both of himself and of his team. He himself was an example of what he required of others.

For the last four years of his ten years at Bermondsey, Bill was also Rural Dean.

He was meticulous – rigorous – almost ruthless in his efficiency. His preaching and his conduct of meetings were always well prepared. His record keeping, not least of his visits, was as meticulous as had been his RAF log book, which itself is one of the most moving documents I have ever handled.

Bermondsey had attracted Bill because he was oriented and disposed towards the under-privileged. In Bermondsey he joined the Labour Party and gave it what local support he could, without making his politics too obvious.

There was an undoubted shyness to Bill. He never let up. So it was not altogether surprising that, after ten years of ministry devoted to Bermondsey, something snapped; and he had a major breakdown. The cause was not simply overwork, indeed, there is no secret about what was the main cause.

Bill was homosexual and knew it. But the Church – and much of the world – at that time did not allow those who were homosexual to be themselves: did not allow *us* who have been created homosexual to have a partner – were we to want one.

At that time, Bill even took the drastic step of having treatment, which some maintained would enable him to stop being who and what he was.

It did not work.

And the courage of him whose courage in the Royal Air Force had been legendary – failed him when he had to face the life that seemed to lay ahead of him.

The tragedy was not only Bill's. It was a tragedy for the Church and for the world; for at that time, the then Prime Minister, Harold Wilson, nominated Bill to be Bishop of Liverpool. He knew, however, he was simply not well enough to accept, and could not undertake such a responsibility.

As I say: the tragedy was not only the tragedy of Bill. And it is a tragedy that, of course, goes on and on in the Church, and in at least *part of* the world.

I'm sure, at this point, Bill would want me to tell you – if only for light relief – a cautionary tale. At Bill's bedside, in the Middlesex Hospital, I met a friend of Bill's from their Clare days – a man who had been happily married for years, and who taught for a time at Eton. He and Bill decided some years ago to go on holiday together but his mother said to him: 'You can't possibly go on holiday with *him*. He's a homosexual.' 'How d'you know?' Bill's friend asked his mother. 'Well,' she said, 'he wears sandals!'

His breakdown laid up Bill for several months. He was clear he could not take on another parish. And some of you know how difficult it is to get a job when, on your record, you have a breakdown.

But Providence was again at hand; and Bill was appointed Director of the Lambeth Endowed Charities. Prior to Bill's appointment, they had been administered by the Rector and churchwardens of St Mary's Church, Lambeth. They were rooted in history – dating back to the eighteenth century. They included some almshouses. They were directly involved with other charities – like the Haberdashers and the Mercers. The Director's job involved the maintenance and care of a whole local estate, and the administration of a very considerable annual income. The charities made some contribution to the life of local schools and to the needs and needy of the area. There was an office to be administered, and the care of the staff who maintained the local estate. The Director had his own flat and garden in a beautiful eighteenth-century house on the Kennington Road.

It was an appointment that might have been designed for Bill at that time. And from 1969, until he retired in 1985, Bill gave himself to the work diligently and wholeheartedly. It required all his gifts of administration, and pastoral skill, and he gave the charities the thorough overhaul which they so desperately needed. His work as the Director of the Lambeth Endowed Charities, added to his ten years experience as Rector of Bermondsey, soon made Bill a man of considerable experience in the field of charitable work.

It is appropriate to record at this point that Bill's introduction to the Coopers' Company in 1942 meant that, he now had much to share with the charitable committee of the Coopers' Company. In 1963 he had been appointed Honorary Chaplain to the Coopers. In 1979 he was elected to the Court. He served as a most distinguished Master from 1985 to 1986. He chaired the charities committee from 1987 until 1996, and was responsible for refocusing the whole ethos of the Company's charitable giving. He served for a whole decade as Governor and Foundation Governor of the Coopers' Company and Coborn School. At the same time, Bill gave great assistance to the charitable work among the homeless that was based on St Botolph's, Aldgate.

Bill was loved by many friends. Yet, for the first ten years of his life in charitable work, he was undoubtedly lonely and, indeed, inwardly angry. But in 1982, by another 'providential accident', Bill met Christopher Eldridge, who was, and is, a landscape architect. *South Pacific* has taught us all something about 'providential accidents': 'Some enchanted evening you may see a stranger across a crowded room'. Bill and Chris soon became partners.

Chris – who himself had had a major breakdown – received a great deal from Bill's friendship, and Bill, in turn, received a great deal from Chris, not least, of course, in these last demanding months and days.

There is no doubt whatever that Bill's last 20 years have been blissfully happy primarily because of his partnership with Chris. It has been a transforming friendship. A lot of what Bill managed to do in his last years he would have found impossible without the support of Christopher. In these last years Bill faced, accepted and rejoiced in his homosexuality. What in earlier life he might have seen as his 'devils' had been transformed by Love.

Bill had always believed in the 'perpetual providence of God' which had so shaped his 'Legion-like' life:

Home and family
Blundell's
Accountancy
The RAF
Trinity Hall
Ormskirk
Clare
Bermondsey
The Lambeth and other charities
The Coopers' Company
His sexuality
Christopher
Cancer

'Providential accidents' can be both positive and negative. And, as with all of us, sometimes Bill's faith in God was tested to and beyond its limits. But Bill had learnt, not least from his friend and mentor, John Robinson, how to live with, for instance, cancer and to continue to believe in the providence of God.

Most of us are here because we want to give thanks to God for the Providence of his gift to us of Bill, and because we want to commit Bill to that perpetual Providence – made most clear in the life and triumphant suffering of Jesus – who yet cried 'My God, my God, why. . .' as at times Bill certainly did.

And it is not only to the Providence of God that we commit our friend Bill. In this Holy Communion, in thankfulness for Bill, we commit ourselves afresh to God's perpetual Providence and Love.

18 'What must I do to win eternal life?': Mark 10: 17–31, St Margaret's, Lee, 12 October 2003

'What must I do to win eternal life?' That's the question at the centre of today's Gospel. I wonder if you could ever imagine yourself asking that question of, say, the Vicar? And I wonder if the Vicar could imagine himself asking that question of, say, the Bishop?

And I wonder: Is it a real question for those of us who gather here today? Because if it isn't, there's no real point in our considering it today. And I think for most people of our world today it isn't a real question ... Though sometimes it becomes real if there's a crisis – if one of the children has a life-threatening illness, or if your husband or wife or partner is taken seriously ill.

Am I right in thinking that most people these days don't think much about things they don't have to consider – until they really have to consider them? 'What must I do to win eternal life?' is not a real question except at 'crisis' times.

Let me share with you something of my own situation at the moment.

I'm 78 and hardly a week goes by without my being asked to take either the funeral of a friend or their memorial service. I never expected that my years of so-called retirement would be so full of friends' funerals. Tuesday this last week I preached in St Paul's Cathedral at the memorial service for Diana Collins, the widow of Canon John Collins of St Paul's. I'd succeeded him as Director of the

Charity Christian Action – which he'd founded. Diana continued to support his work when he died. Next Saturday I preach at the memorial service for Andrew Hake – a priest with whom I served on Faith in the City – the Archbishop's Commission on Urban Priority Areas.

When you take someone's funeral or memorial service, you're bound to ask: 'Where are they now?', and – at 78 you sometimes ask – 'Where shall I soon be?' But that suggests 'eternal life' is something which only begins when this life is finished. There's no doubt that death does make the question of eternal life real – suddenly – for close relatives and friends. 'Where is she now?'

But I don't think that young man, in the Gospel for today, who ran up to Jesus and knelt in front of him, and came out with the question: 'What must I do to win eternal life?' I don't think he had in mind primarily what we call the 'afterlife' – the next world. Nor did Jesus' answer to that question suggest that He was thinking only of the next world in his answer.

Jesus, you'll remember, gave a rather curious answer to the young man. He said: 'Well, you know what the commandments are, don't you?' And the young man in effect says: 'Done those.' And then it says Jesus looked at him, and his heart warmed towards him, and he said to him, 'One thing you lack. Go and sell everything you have and follow me.' And the young man went away depressed because he was loaded: with this world's goods, and it could be that it's that answer which stops some people taking the eternal life question seriously. Because people say to themselves 'I've got a wife and family – or a husband – or aged parents . . . I can't possibly "leave everything" – if that's what eternal life requires, then it's meaningless for me.'

But to go back to the question of bereavement again. Although I wouldn't wish bereavement upon anyone, it's remarkable how many people find that bereavement makes them think about the meaning of life now in a way which they would never have done, had bereavement not come their way. Of course, sometimes bereavement has the opposite effect. It turns a person 'in upon themselves'. But bereavement makes quite a lot of people suddenly sort out their priorities – their priorities in life now.

I think Jesus was saying to that young man something about his priorities. 'Sort out your priorities now – because they're the key to eternal life now.' Eternal life now is about experiencing the love of God now.

The next world – almost by definition – is impossible to describe, or put into words – for the dimensions with which we are familiar in this world – time and space – may not continue as we know them now. As St John says, 'Now are we the sons of God but it *doth not yet appear what we shall be.*' Our future is in the hands of the loving God who, in His love, created us. But now is the time for us to get our priorities right, and the priority above all is to put God's love at the centre of our life: receiving and giving that love.

'What shall I do to win eternal life?' Jesus says, 'Make my love – the giving and receiving of it – your daily priority; your life's priority; and you will win, experience, eternal life now.'

Whenever I hear that Gospel story we had today I always find myself wondering what eventually happened to that young man. When he 'went away sorrowful', was that the end of the affair? The end of his encounter with eternal life? When God gives us freedom he must give us the possibility of rejecting what he offers us – the possibility of going away sorrowful – for good. But I wonder, did that young man retain, say, a memory of the look of Jesus when he warmed to him and looked on him with love?

I have the hope that either that memory, or, maybe, bereavement later in his life, or some other circumstance or that sorrow that we're told he had at the time that 'he went away sorrowful' – caused him later to decide after all to follow Jesus: to alter his priorities.

I asked at the beginning whether that young man's question is real to you. 'What must I do to win eternal life?' I think in the Church we have to ask that question again and again – to ask and answer the question. We have to commit ourselves afresh to the cause of the Kingdom again and again. Indeed, whenever we come to Holy

Communion it's as though we were responding to that question: 'What shall I do to win eternal life?' And we put our hands forward to receive the bread and the wine as our answer to the question. We receive the tokens of God's love for us and make our commitment to that love – to the Kingdom: the Kingdom of Love.

What shall we do to win eternal life? Enter more deeply, more profoundly into communion: into Holy Communion with Christ and one another – for His sake and the sake of His world. But Communion can become a habit. Our Communion hymns can become almost meaningless, or they can be heartfelt commitment to Holy Communion.

If I may return to my own situation again: Communion for me is one of the main ways I keep in touch with those whom I 'love but see no longer'. And some of our hymns express that belief powerfully. I was ordained at Michaelmas – St Michael and All Angels – 52 years ago, so one of my favourite hymns I use often as a prayer, at Communion, but also at home – because it joins earth and heaven in the Kingdom of eternal life is, 'Ye holy angels bright'.

> Ye holy angels bright
>   Who wait at God's command
> Or through the realms of light
>   Fly at your Lord's command,
> Assist our song,
>   For else the theme
>   Too high doth seem
>   For mortal tongue.

19 Memorial Service for Andrew Hake: St Margaret's Church, Oxford, 18 October 2003

It is a very special privilege that Jean has given me, in asking me to preach at Andrew's Memorial Service.

When you're 78, the invitations to preach at your friends' obsequies get – alas! – rather more frequent, but they don't get any easier – if the invitation is not to produce another obituary – in Andrew's case, these have been many and memorable: which is no surprise. But Jean made it clear: she has invited me to *preach* today, yet to relate that preaching to Andrew: his life and his death.

In view of my age, you will not be surprised that I'm an old-fashioned sort of preacher! So I immediately started thinking what should be my text. The answer came quickly: three words: 'Your Kingdom come'. And I chose them, not least because Andrew himself was clearly happy with them when, in 1980, he drafted one section of the report of the Melbourne World Mission Conference, with those very words as the title.

But, of course, the meaning of that word 'kingdom' has been discussed and debated ever since Jesus himself said that the Kingdom had drawn near. St Augustine's great fifth-century work *The City of God* can be thought of as a kind of commentary on 'Your Kingdom come'. But in my lifetime – that's to say, in Andrew's – 'cos he was born only seven weeks before me! – the discussions amongst theologians of the meaning of the phrase have continued apace – from Albert Schweitzer to Andrew's great friend and tutor at Wells Theological College – John Robinson – *Honest to God* Robinson – and, indeed, to the present day. But you needn't worry! I shall not attempt to compete with the theologians today.

I'm going to suggest we start thinking of 'Your Kingdom come' by thinking of *Andrew's* birth – and, if you like, of yours – and mine. The great Victorian theologian, F. D. Maurice, said that, 'Baptism is the proclamation by God that this child is a child of Mine' – not 'will become, at baptism' but is, by birth, a child of Mine – capital 'M'. I can never hold a baby in my arms at a baptism without thinking of that phrase. Childbirth is one of the chief signs of the Kingdom of God that I know. Whatever happens to a child in *later* life it *begins* as a sign of God's Kingdom. Creation reveals the mystery of the kingdom of God; the mystery of the creative power and rule of God.

On this St Luke's Day, it's worth recalling how St Luke tells us: 'They brought young children to Jesus for him to touch, and some of the disciples rebuked them for doing so. But Jesus said "The Kingdom of heaven belongs to such as these".' And I doubt whether anyone here would maintain that he who was baptized Andrew Augustus Gordon had much success in eradicating the signs of the Kingdom of God in him.

Indeed, I suspect that many of us are here today simply because we want to give thanks for the memory of so many ways in which the Kingdom of God seemed to be visible, made manifest, in and through Andrew.

I hardly knew Andrew until 1983: when we began to travel together round more than 30 towns and cities outside London, and spent many hours – and two years – drafting the 38 recommendations to the Church and 32 to the nation, for the Report *Faith in the City*, the product, of course, of the Archbishop's Commission on Urban Priority Areas. By the time our travels together were over, I think I'd got to know what Andrew meant when he said: 'Your Kingdom come'! I could almost hear him saying those words when we stood together in the ghastly surroundings of Strangeways Gaol, Manchester, and on the Meadowell Estate, Newcastle; and in Kirkby, Liverpool. And so on.

I never met a man who was more clear what the Kingdom involved.

And when we were travelling in trains from London to, say, Manchester, where Andrew's friends of Kenya days, Stanley Booth-Clibborn, the Bishop of Manchester, and his wife, Ann, received us, Andrew, on those journeys, would often – in no nostalgic way – share with me how he and Jean had worked for the Kingdom in Kenya. And how he had set it all down in black and white, only six years before, in his book *African Metropolis*. Andrew was clear that the Kingdom involved not only the *churches*, but jobs and health, and schools, and families, and housing, and justice, and relations between races – and involved above all how you related to those you were meeting that very day, whatever their class, or intellect, or cash.

I particularly remember how, when the Commission visited Bradford, we were warmly welcomed by the Muslim Mayor of Bradford. It was somewhat of a surprise for *some* of the Commission. Not so for Andrew. For him it was like being back home in Nairobi. And it was clear to me that day why he'd been invited to join the British Council of Churches' Working Party on Britain as a Multi-Racial Society, as well as the Archbishop's Commission.

In fact, I never heard Andrew speak of Nairobi in the plenary meetings of the Commission. There his authority was primarily what he had been dealing with, for a decade or so, in Swindon, as Social Development Officer. Many of the towns he visited, particularly in the North, had had the heart of them torn out in 're-development' – so-called. Andrew shared with us the enlightened approach to community development alongside economic development which was his experience in Swindon. He was clearly both a prophet and a pastor. He had always new ideas and concepts, and ways of putting them into action, bubbling up inside him, yet he had great care for the 'minute particulars' of social action and for the individuals who would be involved.

Andrew had something of the poet about him as well as the pastor and prophet. R. S. Thomas's poem *The Kingdom* might well have been written by Andrew:

> It's a long way off but inside it
> There are quite different things going on:
> Festivals at which the poor man
> Is king and the consumptive is
> Healed; mirrors in which the blind look
> At themselves and love looks at them
> Back; and industry is for mending
> The bent bones and the minds fractured
> By life. It's a long way off, but to get
> There takes no time and admission
> Is free, if you will purge yourself
> Of desire and present yourself with
> Your need only and the simple offering
> Of your faith, green as a leaf.

When the work of the Archbishop's Commission was over, I was not expecting to see a great deal of Andrew, but by a happy coincidence we were again brought together.

To my surprise and delight, the aged Trevor Huddleston asked me to write his biography, and I began work on it – till a stroke put paid to my doing it. But not until I had visited the place where, in the thirties, Trevor had begun his ministry as a curate – St Mark's, Swindon!! Those who remembered Trevor were, of course, mostly elderly, and often in care. Andrew, typically, was eager to hear the results of my visits to them, and as eager to share with me – and show me – something of what he was now doing in Swindon. It was Jean who pointed out to me that Andrew had gone from one railway town – Nairobi – to another – Swindon.

What was again clear to me in Swindon, as it had been in our journeys round the country, was that Andrew the prophet was also the personal pastor. He knew and was appreciated by literally hundreds of individuals. And they testified to the influence Andrew had had on them. Swindon showed me a little of what life must have been like for Andrew, the prophet and pastor, in Nairobi.

I've already said that Andrew saw the Kingdom not least in terms of families. I have little doubt that he did so in part because of what he received from his own family – from Jean and the children and the grandchildren – and, of course, from his mother and father and his family beginnings.

Now it's too late, there are so many questions I wish I'd asked Andrew. When he might simply have stayed a country man and the son of his father at Stonehays and Yarcombe: who or what was it that called him to serve the cause of the Kingdom in a wider, in a *so much wider*, sphere? Did he first hear the call of the Kingdom as a schoolboy at Marlborough? Or was it as a Captain in the Rifles in the war, serving in Palestine and Egypt?

Something or someone made him decide to read Theology when, as an ex-serviceman, he went up to Trinity College, Cambridge – and you don't get a First Class Honours Degree in Theology unless you're in love with the subject, and work at it.

And Andrew, I would want to ask, when you'd been ordained by Bishop Cockin in 1951 to a housing estate in Bristol, and after a while had become his Social and Industrial Adviser: who or what was it that called you to serve the Kingdom in Kenya? I understand it was my dear friend Janet Lacey, then Director of Christian Aid, who actually persuaded Andrew to accept a post in Kenya. But *why* Andrew left England for Africa is, I'm sure, more complex than simply accepting Christian Aid's invitation – which meant that in 1968 he was seconded to the All African Conference of Churches.

Alas, Andrew, it's too late to ask you now the why and how. All we can say now is: Thank God you prayed 'Your Kingdom come' and followed where you were called.

Maybe if Andrew's last 16 years had taken a somewhat different form, I say to myself, I should have received from Andrew's own lips answers to those questions. For those last sad 16 years I need not only the text 'Thy Kingdom come', I need five more words from the Gospel: 'The *Mystery* of the Kingdom'.

You'll have to forgive the fact – or maybe put up with it – that I often find *Shakespeare* very close to the Gospel. When Lear suggests we 'take upon's the mystery of things as if we were God's spies', I think he comes very close to the Gospel. You can't say 'Your Kingdom come' without encountering the *Mystery* of the Kingdom.

I said earlier that whenever I hold a baby in my arms I think of the birth of that child as a sign of the Kingdom. But it's almost invariably a sign of the mystery of the Kingdom. You never know what's going to become of the child you're baptizing. Did the vicar have any of what would become of Andrew Augustus Gordon when he baptized him in Yarcombe in 1925? I've baptized children who were going to be seriously sub-normal for the rest of their days but I've always said to myself: 'This child is a child of Mine – Capital M'.

In Andrew's last 16 years the ways of God were – God knows – very mysterious. Yet one thing is certain: in all those years Andrew would have wanted us to cleave to the mystery of the Kingdom, which was manifest not least in all those who cared for him.

I suspect I myself would have given up my faith in the Kingdom ages ago had not Jesus Himself cried from the Cross: 'My God, my God, WHY?'. Only a Kingdom that somehow embraces the suffering in the world and includes its mystery will do. Only a Kingdom that somehow faces the fact that we're all created for life *and death* will do, *and* for the mystery of what lies *beyond* death.

It's a kingdom we can of course escape and run away from; but in the end it is the Kingdom of Suffering Love that Andrew has invited us to enter with him.

It was when Andrew was with John Robinson at Wells in 1950 that John produced his first book, entitled *In the End God*. It might have been called *In the End the Kingdom of God*. It might have been called *In the End: The Mystery of the Kingdom of God*. But, in the end, *In the End God* will 'do'.

It was 33 years later that John Robinson asked me to sit next to him in Trinity College Chapel – so familiar to Andrew as an undergraduate – to sit next to him as he preached what he knew to be his last sermon, since he was dying from cancer.

John Robinson asked that at his memorial service the Master of Trinity, the scientist Sir Alan Hodgkin should read a passage by Teilhard de Chardin, the Jesuit scientist and theologian. I think Andrew would be happy were I to read one or two of those paragraphs to end my sermon at his memorial service:

> When the signs of age begin to mark my body (and still more when they touch my mind); when the ill that is to diminish me or carry me off strikes from without or is born within me; when the painful moment comes in which I suddenly awaken to the fact that I am ill or growing old; and above all at that last moment when I feel I am losing hold of myself and am absolutely passive within the hands of the great unknown forces that have formed me; in all those dark moments, O God, grant that I may understand that it is You (provided only my faith is strong enough) who are painfully parting the fibres of my being in order to penetrate to the very marrow of my substance and bear me away within Yourself.
>
> The more deeply and incurably the evil is encrusted in my flesh, the more it will be You that I am harbouring – You as a loving, active principle of purification and detachment. Vouchsafe, therefore, something more precious still than the grace for which all the faithful pray. It is not enough that I shall die while communicating. Teach me to treat death as an act of communion.

'Thy Kingdom come.'

20 The funeral service of Canon Paul Jobson: St Saviour's Pimlico, 7 November 2003

Fifty years ago, when I was a curate next door, at St Stephen's, Rochester Row, I received a telegram from Bishop Cuthbert Bardsley, by then Bishop to the Forces. He was visiting the Forces in Egypt, and the son of the Commander-in-Chief – only six years old – had been taken ill with leukaemia. The telegram asked me to visit the child, Alastair, each day, in the Westminster Hospital, which was then by Lambeth Bridge. After visiting him, I would go into the Chapel of the Hospital, and kneel before the marvellous painting of the Resurrection, by the sixteenth-century Italian artist, Veronese.

Alastair, alas, died. But, over the years, I've returned again and again to kneel before that painting of the Resurrection – now, of course, in the Chapel of the *Chelsea and Westminster* Hospital. I last went there only a fortnight ago, when visiting Paul.

The action of the painting is at night. It's as though the artist wanted us to be fully aware of the darkness that surrounded the Resurrection – the darkness that surrounded and followed the Crucifixion: in which the love of God was made manifest. It is the power of the love of God in Christ which causes him to rise, effortlessly, from the tomb. The darkness cannot overcome the love of God. And Christ strides upwards, His pink cloak, and banner, and accompanying angels, and the radiant aureole around him, all speak of His Easter Triumph.

I was as glad of that painting a fortnight ago as I had been 50 years ago. And I believe it provides the message we need to hear again today.

I begin there. But I begin also with heartfelt thanks for all the wonderful care Paul received from nurses and doctors and all the staff at the Chelsea and Westminster, and from all who cared for Paul in his last days and weeks.

I also find myself thinking thankfully today of all those who helped Paul to be the Paul we knew. His family and his beginnings in East Manchester. He referred so often, and with such affection, to Miles Platting, Manchester. He loved Les Dawson, not least because he echoed his own Manchester beginnings. And our hearts go out today to Kenneth, Paul's brother, who cannot be here today because he is receiving chemotherapy.

I find myself thankful also today for various people who helped Paul as he began his training for ordination: Nicholas Graham of the Community of the Resurrection; Tom Baker, Principal of Wells Theological College, whose funeral Paul felt particularly privileged to conduct in this church just three years ago.

I cannot match the description of Paul as a curate in Woolwich, to be found in his vicar, Nick Stacey's, autobiographical volume *Who Cares?* Nor can I repeat a hundredth – or, indeed, a thousandth of the stories of life at Woolwich which – when he could stop laughing – Paul would still be telling me, over the phone – yet again – until about six weeks ago.

The crypt of the church, that they'd dug out at Woolwich and turned into a wonderful cavern, with superb design and decor, became one of the most successful youth centres in London, due greatly to the gifts of Paul, as well as to his greatly gifted vicar. Discotheques are now a thing of the past. But what Paul achieved with the young people of Woolwich in the Sixties was highly skilled, and imaginative, and the work of a born pastor.

Besides the vicar and the team at Woolwich, Paul was wonderfully cared for by the then Diocesan Director of Post-Ordination Training, Derek Tasker, known affectionately to all, for rather obvious reasons, as 'Tum-Tum'. It was at Woolwich that Paul first began to plan acts of worship for people utterly unused to what went on in churches.

And then, after an action-packed three years, Paul became Chaplain of Culham – the College of Education at Abingdon, Oxford. What he had learnt at Woolwich he shared with Culham students. I've no doubt some are here today: still thankful – 30 years on – for what they received from Paul – not least simply in friendship.

I preached for Paul in Culham in 1972, just when he was about to return to Southwark. I shall never forget the warmth of affection that day that surrounded Paul, from both students and staff.

Then followed his 17 years at Walworth – long years of day-to-day ministry – with hatches, matches and despatches, and training half a dozen or so curates; and, as a teacher said to me: 'He was not only chairman of Governors of the Church School. He was a priest to us all.' Then there was the bar in the crypt – and the unforgettable unforgotten visit of the Queen Mum – when, of course, the lights all failed just before she arrived. But, as she smilingly remarked: 'I expect you've got some candles here.'

When Paul was in intensive care a fortnight ago, three Walworth parishioners arrived. They each had their reason for being grateful for Paul's ministry – but they each represented a thousand – and maybe several thousand – more.

Paul was made an Honorary Canon of Southwark in recognition of his years as Team Rector of Walworth and also his service as Rural Dean.

Bishop Michael Marshall was well aware of Paul's gifts when he was Bishop of Woolwich, and invited Paul to assist him in his new work with the Episcopal Church in America. On his visit, Paul made many lasting friendships. But on his return he was taken very seriously ill, and was in hospital for several weeks, at Canterbury, and had to live with a severely damaged liver for the rest of his life.

It's not easy to get a job in the Church of England when you've had a health breakdown, but Bishop David Jenkins was the Barnabas who took Paul, and gave him the parish of Seaham in the Diocese of Durham. And they became close friends.

In October 1997, I did a BBC *Thought for the Day* about Seaham. Let me quote one or two paragraphs of it:

> Today, I'm going to County Durham, to visit a parish on the coast where the vicar is moving to new work, after eight years of hard labour but rewarding work there.
>
> Parish magazines are often laughed at: but I shall never forget the vicar's letter in that parish magazine, which I read on one of my last visits to the parish, and decided to keep. Here's part of what the Vicar wrote:

> When I came to Seaham, in 1989, the three collieries of the town were still working full shifts and flat out. Within five years, all three had closed down, and their winding shafts and surface buildings wiped from the face of the earth. However, even in 1989 men were being retired early, at the age of fifty.
>
> Although they received large redundancy payments (– and the vicar asked us to note that word –) they felt unwanted, and had lost the only social standing they had in the community. 'He's a miner at Dawdon' people would say or, 'at Vane Tempest', or 'at The Colliery, Seaham'. People were proud to be miners, and the loss of this status was too much for some to live with. Some drank themselves to death; others took their lives by more instant means; the deep waters of the sea, the rope and the overdose. In three years I had conducted the funerals of more suicides than in the previous twenty-five years of my ministry. But others adapted well to leisure and retirement; and the three churches of my parish would not now survive without the voluntary help of such people.
>
> Of course, in eight years the vicar hasn't been able to alter the employment situation in that parish. That's not his primary job – though there are individuals who he has been able to see get appropriate training for work.

Much of the work of the clergy isn't easy to define; but I know this weekend I shall meet many people in that parish who will say they're thankful for the work of their parish priest. He's renewed their ability to be hopeful, their capacity to care for one another, their sense of belonging to one another; but above all, their sense of purpose in life. And people with such gifts can never be 'redundant'.

And so to St Saviour's.

Those of you who worship here regularly will know that the planning of the worship was Priority No. 1 for Paul – and the beautifying of the church, so that the worship would be what Paul believed it should be, was also 'top priority'.

The Ascension was Paul's favourite feast of the Church – and he believed that all the worship of the Church should reflect the glory of the Ascended Christ. 'Glory' was one of Paul's favourite words.

What more shall I say? Need I say more? Yes – there are one or two things more I need to say.

First: Paul's huge gift of humour. And anyone who hasn't a sense of humour should switch off for a minute or two!

Paul came on the phone to me about a couple of months ago. Paul adored Oscar Wilde and sometimes he would phone and speak almost entirely in the voice of Edith Evans as Lady Bracknell. This particular morning it was obvious he was very pleased with something he'd just written – and wanted to share it. It was something in the style of Noel Coward – and I'm very grateful to those who managed to recover it from Paul's computer. Here it is!!

> Mr Irving Berlin often emphasises sin in a charming way
> Noel Coward wrote a song or two to show sex was here to stay;
> Richard Rodgers, it's true, took a more romantic view of
>   that slight biological urge –
> Bit it really was Cole who conspired to make the whole
>   thing merge.

He said

Bearded orthodox Greeks do it
Nice young men who sell antiques do it -
Let's do it – let's fall in love.

Bishops wearing purple socks do it
St Stephen's House in designer frocks do it
Let's do it – let's fall in love.

George Carey feels that he must do it –
Andrew, his son, can just do it.
Let's do it – let's fall in love.

Lady Brentford can't quite do it
    She's so highly strung;
The Bishop of Liverpool might do it –
    But he looks far too young.

Mrs C F Alexander did it
    But she did it in verse
The Dean and Chapter of St Paul's do it
    But they have to rehearse.

At HTB some of the men do it –
Others say a prayer and then do it.
Let's do it – let's fall in love.

General Synod en bloc does it
Church House staff by the clock do it
Let's do it – let's fall in love.

Archdeacons and rural deans do it
They long to have machines to do it –
Let's do it – let's fall in love.

That was Paul loving being Paul – only six weeks or so before he died.
And today we thank God for every bit of Paul: not least, of course, the
Paul who so loved his dogs.

But there's one more subject I must mention – and it's a very difficult subject. Most of us have subjects we cannot mention – or find it difficult to mention – even to our best friends. And friends – if they are friends – are particularly reluctant to presume on that friendship, and invade, or lecture us. I was never able to discuss one subject with Paul, and that was alcohol – drink. Or, rather, I wasn't able to talk about it – until very recently.

I decided to call on Paul at the Vicarage late one afternoon – after he'd begun to look very ill – let's say a couple of months ago.

He suddenly told me he'd just had a 'wonderful afternoon' – visiting a bereaved parishioner whose husband he'd recently buried. 'What was so wonderful about it?' I asked. He took a long time to answer. Then he said: 'Well, her husband had died because of the demon drink. And she wanted to tell me how awful she now felt – because she'd gone on at him about his drinking. And it was no good. "He still went on drinking – and I still went on being angry with him," she said. "And now I feel so guilty and ashamed."'

Paul looked at me and said: 'I just told her I understood. I understood her desire to shout at him – and I understood his not being able to give up the drink. I understood how he felt and how she felt. And she suddenly looked happy – as though she'd been forgiven.'

Paul looked straight at me again and said: 'You understand what I'm trying to say to you, don't you?' 'Yes, Paul,' I said: 'I do.'

'He saved others: himself he could not save' – though Paul did not touch alcohol for his last 14 years.

Jesus understood – understands – Paul as no one on earth understood him. And the Jesus portrayed in that painting in the Chapel in the Chelsea and Westminster has now taken Paul to be with Him.

As one of Paul's favourite Ascensiontide hymns says:

> Thou hast raised our human nature
>> On the clouds to God's right hand:
> There we sit in heavenly places
>> There with thee in glory stand:

Jesus reigns adored by angels
Man with God is on the throne
Mighty Lord in thine ascension
We by faith behold our own.

Today we entrust our friend Paul into the care of Christ, Risen, Ascended, Glorified.

21 How to look: The Chapel Royal, St James's Palace, 4 January 2004

Peter Brook – probably the greatest producer of Shakespeare of our time – had to give a lecture recently, at which it was the custom always for the lecturer to light a candle before giving the lecture. He said: 'In a way, now the candle is alight, there is nothing more to say. If we could only sit and watch, feel and understand this extraordinary miracle, words would be superfluous . . . If only we knew how to look.'

Well, it's, of course, the custom for *us* to light *two* candles – at least – before our service. And we light many more at Christmas, 'If only we knew how to look.'

Today I simply want to share with you some of the thoughts that have come to me as I have dwelt on those words of Peter Brook.

First: whenever we see a candle lit, we need to be aware that we are in the presence of a great mystery – a profound mystery. In *King Lear* – as Peter Brook, of all people, would know well – Lear says: 'We must take upon's the mystery of things as if we were God's spies.' Well, whenever a candle is lit, we must take upon us the mystery and miracle of Light in Darkness – 'as if we were God's spies'.

In a way, it's what we might call a 'natural' mystery. It reflects and echoes that first great creative moment when God said: 'Let there be light; and there was light' – that moment that Haydn so marvellously portrays in *The Creation*.

St Paul says: 'First that which is natural; then that which is spiritual.' And the first truth that lies behind the lighting of a candle is that truth of nature without which all of us would perish. We need light to live at all: to survive. But Light and Creation – Light and Life – are only the beginning of the mystery.

When we light a candle, there's a second meaning of the mystery which is never far away. Again, Shakespeare puts it into words, in *Macbeth*. Macbeth himself says: 'Out, out brief candle . . .' When a candle is lit, we are not only near to the mystery of mystery and miracle of Light in Darkness, we are very near to the very mystery of Time itself – and thus the mystery of each one of us. The brevity of our life is displayed in the brief life of a candle.

There are a good many phrases which suggest that we will do anything but learn to look: to sit still and contemplate that mystery. And none is better than the familiar phrase 'to burn the candle at both ends'. To sit still and watch a candle burn is to see the mystery of Time; the mystery of Life; the mystery of ourselves.

But there's another aspect of the mystery in that ancient legal phrase: 'Bell, book and candle'. The candle there refers to our human capacity for truth – or falsehood: for making responsible human judgements. In other words: for making acts of faith, and belief, and trust.

The alternative is posed starkly in *Macbeth*:

> Out, out, brief candle!
> Life's but a walking shadow . . .
> It is a tale
> Told by an idiot, full of sound and fury,
> Signifying nothing.

The candle speaks of truth, and meaning, and faith, that issues in prayer; and of Light in Darkness. Hence we light candles as prayers.

The Psalmist says, in Psalm 18.v.28:

> Thou also shalt light my candle
> The Lord God shall make my darkness to be light.

And the writer of the Book of Proverbs declares:

>The spirit of man is the candle of the Lord.

But all I have said so far, however important, is only a preface and a preliminary to what I must now say.

We light candles at Christmas because, as the Christian Gospel proclaims, in Christ 'was life, and the life was the light of men. And the light shineth in darkness, and the darkness comprehended it not': could not master it, overcome it, eclipse it, extinguish it.

Some of you, I imagine, will have been privileged to have attended one of the most moving services of the Church called 'Tenebrae', which, of course, simply means 'darkness'. It's held in many monasteries, and held in darkness – on the last days of Holy Week, and is really a prolonged visual meditation on the events of the first Holy Week – the Betrayal; the Judgement; the Crucifixion; and the burial of Christ. A row of candles is lit – and extinguished one by one. A psalm is chanted between the extinguishing of each candle – until the final candle is extinguished, and all depart in silence; and there is 'darkness over all the earth'.

The extinguished candle symbolizes Christ the Victim: the Light snuffed out; and symbolizes Christ alongside all victims. That's quite a thought this particular week – with all the victims of the earthquake in Iran.

But then, on Easter day, at dawn, a candle, the Paschal Candle, is lit and raised on high; and a lone voice sings 'The Light of Christ' – *Lumen Christi*. And the Easter Candle triumphantly proclaims the full truth of the Light of the World.

If you go to stay at a Franciscan friary, as like as not you will be woken early by a friar, knocking at your door and saying 'Christ be thy Light'. (In my time, I've heard some very irreverent responses to that early morning greeting!) At the beginning of a New Year, 'Christ be thy Light' is as powerful a greeting as at the beginning of a new day. All that I've said so far – and more – is there when we learn to look at a candle being lit.

In a sense, I've said all I've got to say. But, at 78, as a priest, I spend much of my time attending and taking the funerals and memorial services of my friends . . .; and I confess I need – I rather desperately need – to hear what the candle has to say about, for instance, my friend Paul, the Vicar of St Saviour's, Pimlico, at whose funeral I preached only a few weeks ago. I'd known him since he was ordained 40 years ago. Then there's Bernard – who died after he'd sent me his Christmas card this year.

Well, there's a very precious promise in the Book of the Revelation of St John the Divine; and I pass it on to you – especially to those of you who have been bereaved:

> And they need no candle, neither the light of the sun,
> for the Lord God giveth them light.

I want also to say to you: 'Do not think of the darkness as without God.' The Psalmist says: 'The darkness is no darkness with thee. The darkness and the light to thee are both alike.' A hero of mine, C. F. G. Masterman, a victim of depression, has that text on his memorial, carved by Eric Gill. 'The darkness is no darkness with thee.'

But on the first Sunday of the New Year, I'm not going to end with another world than this. I'm going to go back to my childhood – for 'except ye become as little children you cannot enter the kingdom of heaven' – and candles make us all remember our childhood. Children – and the child in us now – can appreciate candles probably more than the grown-up.

Candles make me remember my Methodist Sunday School, and my mother teaching me to sing – 70 and more years ago:

> Jesus bids us shine with a clear pure light
> Like a little candle burning in the night
> In this world of darkness, so we must shine
> You in your small corner, and I in mine.

At the beginning of a New Year, I don't think we should despise Jesus bidding us shine 'like a candle burning in the night'. And if you should prefer Shakespeare, there's always Portia in *The Merchant of Venice*:

> How far that little candle throws his beams!
> So shines a good deed in a naughty world.

All I have said could be summed up by saying, 'I don't think – at the beginning of a New Year – we can afford to ignore amongst our resolutions Peter Brook's words "If only we knew how to look".'

And, when we look, we shall realize that the candle is simply a symbol, and so too is the Light. They are both symbols of what Dante called 'the Love that moves the sun and the other stars' for God is Love.

22 'The trumpet shall sound ... and we shall be changed': 1 Corinthians 15:52, BBC Radio 4 Sunday Worship, St Martin-in-the-Fields, 8 February 2004

First Address

'We shall be changed.' Those were the four last words we heard of that marvellous solo from Handel's *Messiah*. If you're 78 – as I am – you can claim to know quite a bit about change. The danger is you claim to know too much about it and become a bit of a bore on the subject. 'D'you know? When I was a boy...' is quickly succeeded by 'D'you know? When I was thirty...' And so on. The simple fact is that, in the Providence of God, the world never stops changing; and, if you live long enough, you're bound to have experienced a great deal of change.

A few years ago, I had to preach a University Sermon at Oxford. After the sermon, as I descended the pulpit steps, a young blonde came out of the congregation, and suddenly flung her arms round me, and said: 'Eric, you don't know how marvellous it is to see you.'

At first, I hadn't a clue who she was, but then, in a split second, I realized that the last time I'd seen her, she was a *man*.

Not just to dismiss her, I said: 'Half-past two at the Randolph Hotel.' Then I joined the Vice-Chancellor's Procession.

The Vice-Chancellor – Lord Neill – said to me quietly, while we were processing down the centre aisle, in our 'glad rags': 'Eric, I don't immediately think of you as someone whom blondes are forever throwing themselves at . . .' I took a few more steps, and then said: 'Supposing I told you that the last time I saw that blonde she was male – what would you say?' 'I'd say "typical,"' said Lord Neill, with a smile. And then, as we moved further down the aisle, he said: 'May I tell the ladies that, when we join them for coffee?' 'Yes,' I said. 'But don't make too much of a joke of it. That blonde's gone through hell, and so has the person who was her partner.'

In fact, the head of the College where my blonde friend was studying, was at coffee; and she knew my friend well; and reported she was doing well at her studies, and was happy with College life, as I discovered for myself when I met her – as arranged – at the Randolph Hotel. That blonde is now, in fact, thinking of ordination. And her former partner, thanks to the care of many, is running a centre for prayer and worship. There's change for you! Sex change – change in Oxford – and in society – and in the Church. Change that has taken time, and for which there has been quite a price to be paid.

How do we face change?

First: by saying to ourselves: 'He's got the whole world in his hands.' Change does not belong to someone else.

So, second: we shall look for God in the changed situation. It's still God's world. We respond to events within God's world. Of course, that doesn't mean that all change will reveal God. Far from it! But it does mean we must expect surprises. And some of our most strongly held beliefs may turn out to be prejudices.

And we shall be surprised to meet God in the new situation: in a changed situation – when we may have thought we were leaving him behind.

Not only the situation will have changed, but – as we heard at the beginning – 'We shall be changed.'

Second Address

There's nothing like change for testing what we really believe in. The idea of 'what's good and true' is tested by change. 'I much prefer what we had before' we say. Or: 'Yes. I think that's a real improvement.' We make changes because we believe the change will make things better.

The Church of St Martin-in-the-Fields butts onto Trafalgar Square; and, as you probably know, the layout of the Square has recently been radically changed because people – rightly or wrongly – thought the new layout would be better for all. (Though every London taxi driver has his own opinion on that!)

The fact is, we all live our lives continually with the possibility – and more than just the possibility – of change. Each of us, by being human, has a stake in changing our country and our world. We may also have some share in the change in the world of our work, and in our family life.

We have to be educated and trained for all sorts of changes that confront us; and trained to make changes. But all that requires that we shall face the underlying, basic question of what we believe in, and what will be for our own good, and the good of our family, our neighbourhood, our country, and our world.

The changing world forces us to reflect on what is required of us. The pressure of change may sometimes make us want to cry out: 'Stop the world: I want to get off!' But the world never stops, and the possibility and actuality of change never stop.

And to age is, of course, to change. And that happens to us all – whether we like it or not.

And, of course, we all face the final change – which is death itself. At my age, I'm surrounded by the sickness – and often death – of my friends of many years. And the final phase of change requires final acts of faith.

It was the Jewish prophet, Micah, who put the memorable question: 'What does the Lord require of you, but to do justly, and to love mercy, and to walk humbly with your God?' Eight centuries later, Jesus called his disciples to follow him along that way. It's something we all still need to face, if we're not simply to be caught up in change – without being able to influence it.

St Martin-in-the-Fields has to re-equip itself to be a church that can really help people, in the midst of this world of change.

But the challenge is to each one of us: to examine the roots of our faith: whatever that faith may be. That's certainly one of the most important steps any of us can take.

And many of us would want to say that – as we face the realities of change and face the question of belief – we go on discovering more and more of the God who loved us into existence, and who, we now believe, will be with us wherever life carries us: who will be alongside us, in all the changing scenes of life – and beyond.

23 Memorial service for Daniel George Goyder: St Mary-le-Tower, Ipswich, 22 March 2004

I count it a great privilege that Jean has given me, in inviting me to preach at Dan's Memorial Service.

It's clear that not only those of us gathered here, but a host of others, were shocked by the news of Dan's death; and, besides commemorating his life, which others have done so movingly today, I must endeavour to address the subject of the bereavement that his death has caused Jean, and the family, and, indeed, so many of us.

I had, at most, a minute with Dan at his retirement party at King's College, London, last autumn, and only brief conversations with him on the phone when he was ill. My last long conversation with Dan was, in fact, when I preached at the Patronal Festival of St Edmundsbury Cathedral, on the Feast of St James, last July, when both Dan and Jean were present. Dan showed then no signs whatever of what lay ahead of him – indeed, he looked as young as ever.

The seventeenth-century nonconformist divine, Richard Baxter – who wrote *Ye holy angels bright* – said that the preacher should preach as a 'dying man to dying men'. I have always tried to bear those words in mind. And when, after Dan's death, I read again what I had said from the Cathedral pulpit last July – and realized that they were virtually my last words to Dan, I was not unhappy with them – if there had to be 'last words'. And I shall share some of my thoughts then with you today.

I took my text from St Paul's First Letter to the Corinthians: Chapter 4, Verse 1: 'We are to be regarded as the ministers of Christ and stewards of the mysteries of God.' I chose as the first mystery which we have to steward, the mystery of Time.

Last July there was no need – in that great and historic cathedral – to argue the point. But neither is there today. We are all too conscious now of Dan's 65 years – no more: no less – through which he was a blessing to us all.

The mystery of Time is manifest to me when I remember my first meeting with Dan. It was 1956. Dan had just come up from Rugby School to Trinity College, Cambridge, where I was then Chaplain. And that's where our nearly 50 years friendship began. When Dan left Trinity, in 1959, so did I; and, for a year, Dan came to live in St George's Vicarage, in Camberwell – the Trinity College Mission, in inner South London – where I was then Vicar and Warden.

I have many memories of that time. My housekeeper, Mrs Swinburne, simply adored Dan. Today, just one memory of those days must suffice.

One evening, Dan's father came to dinner. I knew him well as George Goyder. We both served on the Church Assembly and the General Synod of the Church of England. That evening, George sat on my right, with Dan next to him. George said suddenly: 'You know: Dan and I have never had a cross word, have we, Dan?' 'No, father,' said Dan. But he winked at me after his reply – and smiled. I associate that wink with Dan; for he used it often in life – with his memorable and characteristic smile.

Not all that long ago, I had a meal in London one evening with Dan, before going on to the English National Opera. In recent years it had become a habit of ours. It was a relaxed evening – as though we had 'all the time in the world'.

We never went to Gilbert and Sullivan; but part of me now wishes we'd gone to *The Yeoman of the Guard* some time, and heard Gilbert's marvellous verse:

Is life a boon?
  If so, it must befall
  That Death, whene'er he call,
Must call too soon.

A few days ago, I took out my marriage file; and there was the service sheet of Dan and Jean's marriage, which I was privileged to conduct, at St Mary's, Saffron Walden, 28 July 1962. It seemed but yesterday. I noted that even then we were singing 'Yea, though I walk through death's dark vale, Yet will I fear no ill'.

Dan and Jean had an idyllic marriage – blessed with the gift of four children: Joanna, Elizabeth, Andrew and Richard, and grandchildren. But, as Hotspur says, in *Henry IV*: 'Gentlemen: The time of life is short.'

It helps me on occasions such as this, to remind myself that Jesus died – was killed – when he was 33. What a time that must have been for Joseph and Mary and for the rest of Jesus' family and friends.

The Mystery of Time. It's an unplumbable mystery.

But there's a second great mystery of God we have to steward: the Mystery of Place.

G. K. Chesterton said: 'For anything to be real it must be local.'

It's clear from what has been said today, and from what has been written about Dan, that, over the years, he was a man of many localities.

Henley, Rugby, Cambridge, Camberwell;
Harvard and Berkeley;
Capel St Mary and Ipswich;
The offices of the Monopolies and Mergers Commission just
    behind the Law Courts.
and of Allan & Overy,
and of Birketts,
and Linklaters,
and of the Eds and Ips Board of Finance;

King's College, London,
The University of Essex,
The University of East Anglia,
The University of Cambridge.

to say nothing of much loved places of family holidays.

The Mystery of Time and the Mystery of Place are inseparable for all of us from the third great mystery, the Mystery of Persons.

When I think of Dan as husband – or father – or grandfather – or friend – or practising – or teaching – competition law, or as an honorary Lay Canon of St Edmundsbury & Ipswich – Time and Place and Person seem – most often – as they are – almost inseparable. They become part of the one mystery of Being who we are: the mystery of who Dan was – and is – in the loving care of God.

Shakespeare invites us to 'take upon's the mystery of things as if we were God's spies'. Particularly on such a day as this I like the idea that God has invited us to be one of his spies.

As a close friend of Dan for nearly 50 years it was a particular privilege to be allowed to 'spy out' what made him the person he was and to conclude, after all those years, that he had utter integrity. But he had even more than that. He was blessed with an almost innate sense of the love of God: an unshakeable belief in the love of God, which stayed with him, even at the approach of Death.

Death – and especially untimely death – makes most of us ask afresh the great questions, not only about Death, and what lies beyond it, but about life. Is there, in the end, any meaning to it?

Dan never doubted the love of God. And no one could accuse him of being simple, or thoughtless. On the contrary.

When I think of Dan and Jean's first meeting, I don't immediately want to reach for my Bible. I think of *South Pacific*:

> Some enchanted evening
> You may see a stranger
> Across a crowded room . . .

139

And from that moment, life is never the same again.

I've no doubt that for Jean that moment is 'unforgettable, unforgotten'.

Anyone who runs away from the mystery of such moments runs away from one of the most important ingredients of our humanity.

The Mystery of Time, the Mystery of Place, and the Mystery of Persons all come together at such moments; and we have to 'steward' such moments through the spiritual gifts of our humanity. I have already mentioned the Mystery of Death, and what lies beyond it. But today I mustn't just mention it and leave it at that. Nor must I pretend I have easy answers – or simply take refuge in that beautiful word 'mystery'.

The problem we have to face today is that that 'enchanted' evening which brought Dan and Jean together has now been followed – 40 years on – by cruel evenings and nights and days which have now seemingly separated them – and us. And it won't do simply to credit God with the 'enchanted evening' but not the others.

One of my favourite texts comes from St John's Gospel. Jesus simply says to Simon Peter: 'What I do thou knowest not now but thou shalt know hereafter.' We're not to be 'know-alls' in this life; but we are to be people of faith.

I myself believe that the Love which was manifest in Dan's creation – and indeed in his life – has not finished with him – or with us.

And I believe that, not least, because the Creator's Love, which was manifest in Jesus, did not come to an end with His death.

You will not be surprised to hear that this is not the first time I have had to preach at the untimely death of a close friend from cancer.

My meeting with Dan at Trinity College, Cambridge, has reminded me of the death of my friend Bishop John Robinson, who died – at 64 – of cancer. Bishop John, then Dean of Trinity, asked me to sit next to him in the Chapel at Trinity – so well known to Dan – when John preached his last sermon there. And he asked me to be ready to take over from him, he was so ill, if he couldn't go on with the sermon.

I had to learn that sermon of John Robinson's almost off by heart, and some sentences of it I can never forget. John Robinson – biblical scholar, theologian, and author of the best-seller significantly called *Honest to God* – said in his last sermon: 'One of the features of my sort of cancer is that one usually gets no warning until it's too late.' And then he said: 'God is to be found in the cancer as in everything else. If he is not, then he is not the God of the Psalmist who said: "If I go down into Hell, Thou art there also" – let alone of the Christian, who knows God most deeply in the Cross.'

I do not apologize for asking you to think at Dan's memorial service about these mysteries of God. I have no doubt Dan would be very happy if his memorial service had made all his family and friends, and fellow workers, who had gathered together in thanksgiving for him – if his death had made us think afresh of the mystery – the mysteries – of life and death, and what it means to steward those mysteries of God: of Time and Place and Persons.

And I think he would be very happy if, as part of the mystery of Love – not least love for him – we were to commend him to the Love which created him; to the Love that blessed him as he went about his way in this world; and – some of us believe – even now blesses him as he goes on his way.

And, in so doing, we shall be thanking God that Dan was himself such a marvellous 'minister of Christ and a steward of the mysteries of God'.

24 Sung Evensong for the 175th King's College Anniversary Alumni Weekend: The Chapel of King's College, London, 11 June 2004

Philippians 1.3: 'I thank my God on every remembrance of you.'

I don't think I'm presuming or assuming too much, if I credit those attending a weekend for College Alumni – and attending Sung Evensong in Chapel – with, let's say, a degree of thankful remembrance. It's our memories, to a considerable extent, that will have brought us back to this place.

The older I get – and I'm now in my eightieth year – the more I realize that one of the most important parts of our humanity is our memory. As Marcel Proust wrote: 'Even though our lives wander, our memories remain in one place.' Yet, really, it's very difficult to say what memory is.

We talk of having a 'good' memory, so that we can recall particular events, and particular people. Yet what is memory? It's nothing like a toe or a tooth that can be touched. It's more an activity than an object; or, rather, it's a vast number of complex inter-related activities and processes.

The *Oxford Dictionary*, rather disappointingly, defines memory as 'The faculty by which things are remembered: this faculty considered as residing in a particular individual.' Nevertheless, I want to invite you to be thankful for the marvel and mystery of those processes of memory, without which it would be impossible for any of us to confront or, indeed, to understand life itself. Let each of us thank God for our memory: for our basic memory processes: learning, recalling, retaining, forgetting, and so on.

Wonder is the gateway to worship – wonder, not least, at the marvel of our gifts, our everyday gifts – the way we've been created. And I believe we need particularly to wonder at the gift of memory: our memory, which, I've suggested, has played a considerable part in bringing us together today.

Part of the gift of memory is the gift that enables us to select what to remember. We can't possibly remember everything that comes on to what I will call the screen of our memory – every minute: every second – yet, somehow, we remember some things: some persons. We eliminate all but a special selection, so as not to be overwhelmed and confused by a mass of memories. That gift of selection is part of the marvel of memory. So we all arrive here today with our clutch of memories: not least, of this place.

I was the last of four children and left school at 14, when the Second World War broke out. I worked for several years on London's riverside, on Bankside, where now the Globe Theatre stands; and learnt the organ at Southwark Cathedral in my lunch hours – before I eventually came to King's, after seven years of war-time work.

My first experience of King's was through evening classes, by which I hoped to gain admission to King's full-time. I had to learn Greek and Latin from scratch, amongst other things. Characteristically, the new Dean of King's – in 1946 – Eric Abbott, had decided to take the New Testament Greek evening class himself.

We met in his room, close to the Chapel. Half a dozen of us sat round his large table, whilst he walked round it, and us, in academic gown, with his mortarboard in his hand. He began, of course, at the beginning, with the alphabet. I remember how embarrassed and tongue-tied I was in such utterly unfamiliar academic surroundings.

He went round to see what each of us had written; and when he saw that I had put a dot on an iota, he bent down and whispered quietly 'Dot not.' And, as he said the words, to give them emphasis, and in mock rebuke, touched me gently on the head, twice, with his mortarboard.

Down the arches of the years – nearly 60 of them – I still remember that evening, and that touch. It was the beginning of a friendship that lasted till his death, nearly 40 years later. And 'I thank my God on every remembrance' of Eric Symes Abbott.

But almost as soon as I speak of the wonder of memory, and how appropriate it is to be thankful for it, here and now I find myself also wanting to say something about the suffering that can be related to memory – not least to loss of memory.

We will all be aware that this very day President Reagan is being buried, after years of Alzheimer's disease: and most people of my age, these days, are just a bit scared that Alzheimer's will take their memory away. And without our memory we will be virtually without our identity.

But there are, of course, other aspects of memory which are painful to recall. The marvel of memory is that, paradoxically, it sometimes introduces us to very powerful experiences of things which we would rather forget. Because guilt and memory go together, guilt, memory and forgiveness need also to be brought together.

Some people bear for life the memory of rejection in childhood. So depression and memory are often closely associated. Others remember, for years, the death of a parent or of a child, or of a friend. True religion will always relate to and deal directly with our memories.

I was very glad to read Theology here at King's. But it was not reading Theology as an academic subject which primarily made my faith come alive.

And when I hear verses of Scripture these days, they do not only bring to my mind academic theology. They are more likely to remind me of incidents in the last 50 or 60 years – in my own life and experience, or in situations in which I have been involved. Sometimes they invoke a response within me. Often, certainly, the memory is involved in one way or another.

The words of the malefactor on the cross, crucified beside Christ, become, for instance, a heartfelt prayer: 'Lord, remember me when thou comest into thy kingdom.'

Or the words that Johann Sebastian Bach so marvellously – and memorably – set to music in the St Matthew Passion: 'Peter remembered the words of Jesus: Before the cock crow thou shalt deny me thrice. And he went out and wept bitterly.' Those words seldom fail to stir depths within one.

Or my text today 'I thank my God on every remembrance of you' – becomes a prayer which I find myself uttering again and again concerning friend upon friend.

Or, say, the verses from the Psalms; 'Remember how short my time is' becomes a direct message to the heart.

'Remember Jesus Christ, risen from the dead' becomes not just a Pauline phrase, in his letter to Timothy, but a kind of personal instruction.

And there's that remarkable command of Jesus: 'If thou bring thy gift to the altar, and there remember that thy brother hath ought against thee, leave there thy gift before the altar, and go thy way: first be reconciled to thy brother.'

Then there's the brief simple instruction that lies at the heart of the Holy Communion: 'Do this in remembrance of me.'

The consecration of memory is something of huge importance in Christian faith and practice.

Yet I would not have you believe that when I left here I was an example of Anglican piety. Far from it!

And, as I think again, on my text 'I thank my God on every remembrance of you' I want to give you just one more example of what King's has meant to me, which took my memory far beyond the bounds of the Church of England, and still does.

I used to sit each day in Chapel in the same place: against the West Wall. One day I noticed the memorial on the wall above me. It's still there. It's in affectionate memory of Samuel Rabbeth MD, London. Born August 19th 1858 Died October 1884. The memorial tells how he entered the medical faculty of King's, having been earlier at King's College School: how he was Scholar and Gold Medallist of the University of London; how he became House Physician at King's College Hospital, and then went on to be Senior Resident Officer at the Royal Free Hospital. And then, on 10 October 1884, he contracted diphtheria by sucking the tracheotomy tube, in the hope of saving the life of a child with diphtheria. The memorial says: 'The self-sacrifice of his death answered to the unselfishness of his life.' I thank my God on every remembrance of him.

Samuel Rabbeth sounds like a Jewish name. His memorial may, of course, be in this Chapel because he was a Christian Jew. It matters not. The self-sacrifice of a fellow human being has been to me a powerful example over the years – and I've no doubt to others.

In the end it's our humanity that counts.

I thank my God for every remembrance of Samuel Rabbeth – as I thank God for the gift of memory itself: not least the rich memories with which this College has furnished me from 1946 until now.

25 The fiftieth anniversary of the ordination of the Revd John Baker: St Luke's, Battersea, 4 July 2004

On this rather special occasion of the fiftieth anniversary of the ordination of our mutual friend – and your Honorary Curate – John Baker, I have two texts for you: The first: 1 Corinthians 4:1: 'Let a man so account of us as of the ministers of Christ, and stewards of the mysteries of God.' And the second: Luke 10:27: 'You shall love the Lord your God with all your heart, and with all your soul, and with all your strength, and with all your mind; and your neighbour as yourself.'

Twenty-five years ago – in 1979 – I had to be responsible for a conference of the clergy of the Diocese of St Albans. I edited a small book in preparation for it, called *Stewards of the Mysteries of God*. Those preparatory papers were by a variety of people, including a poet; and the head of the social services of a big city, who was also a priest; and theologians, and parish priests. We met for the conference in Canterbury, and our bishop, Robert Runcie, then Bishop of St Albans, had only just been appointed Archbishop of Canterbury. Twenty-five years ago we knew we needed to think afresh together what it means to be 'Stewards of the Mysteries of God.'

A fortnight ago, I went away for three days to St Mary's Abbey, West Malling, to think out – yet again – the meaning of that phrase. The situation in our country today has radically changed from what it was 25 years ago. Several theological colleges, for instance, are at this moment threatened with closure.

The first engagement I had when I returned from the Abbey at West Malling was a particular delight. It was to have John Baker to tea. I wanted to spend an hour or so with him , talking about his last 50 years as a 'steward of the mysteries of God' – and what those 50 years of priesthood had meant to him.

The next day, Saturday, I had to go to St Paul's Cathedral, for the ordination of a young friend, who is also a teacher. He asked me to stand with him when he was ordained. It's the custom in London Diocese to have supporters stand with you when you make the ordination promises. As it happened, it meant standing virtually on the spot where I myself had knelt 53 years ago – when I was ordained deacon.

When I had my tea-time chat with John, he was kind enough to give me a copy of the talk, or lecture, which he'd given here a month ago, entitled 'Hearts and Minds', which led me to take as my second text: 'You shall love the Lord your God with all your heart, and with all your soul, and with all your strength, and with all your mind, and your neighbour as yourself.'

I found it particularly moving to read in John's talk that his father had been unemployed for two years in the Depression – and was, indeed, unemployed when John was born, in 1929; and his Dad was determined that John should never be reduced to working as a factory hand, as he had done; and when he spotted an advert in the local paper in Bristol, advertising auditions for a choral scholarship, he put John in for it, and much to their surprise and delight, he got it. So it was to All Saints Choir School, Clifton, Bristol that John went for his education for nine years – singing as a bass in his last year. John was there right through the war, and when the church was bombed they moved into the church hall. John cycled to and from school; and they sang Evensong every day, except Wednesdays, when they had games.

John is clear that his thoughts about ordination had their beginnings in that education, and in those who taught him and befriended him at the school, and later at Oxford.

His first contacts with Bishop Mervyn Stockwood were probably when he was at the Choir School, which was a parish fairly near to where Mervyn was then vicar.

I never cease to be surprised at the very varied stories which people tell you when you ask them how they came to get ordained. One thing is certain: that all of us here today are very glad and thankful that John was ordained.

In fact, when we were discussing together what ordination meant to John, we spent some time musing on the fact that few jobs give you more opportunity to come close to other people – in very different jobs and situations. To use John's words: the priesthood gives you huge opportunities to have regard for other people: to value them, and see their significance and importance.

It often seems to me that those who are ordained divide roughly into two groups: those who wordlessly seem to proclaim: 'I am ordained ... I am a priest', and those who recognize in others their priesthood, and see it as the work of an ordained priest to help other people to discover their priesthood – whatever particular job in the world they may in fact be called to do.

Outside St Paul's Cathedral, before and after the ordination last Saturday week, there was a huge crowd of people; and you could see immediately that some clergy were intent on proclaiming by their dress that they were priests and were very distinguishable – coming through the streets to the Cathedral in their cassocks and in some cases wearing what we used to call a 'shovel hat'. (As W. S. Gilbert might have said: 'Clergy in their shovel hats were plentiful as tabby cats – in point of fact, too many.') John would never have been numbered among such clergy. He has not been amongst those who wanted to increase the distance between him and those not ordained. He has wanted to help people discover their priesthood, whatever their job in life.

So I thankfully repeat my first text: 'We are members of Christ, and stewards of the mysteries of God.' Every human being is potentially that by their very creation and their humanity. And John has seen it as his job as a priest to remind people of that by his regard for them and care for them.

Let us just look at that text a little more closely. What are the mysteries of God we all have to steward? Well, they are many. Today I select just two.

Time and Place.

John has spent all his ministry in Battersea, apart from his second curacy, in Richmond. He was incumbent at All Saints Battersea from 1962 until 1993. G. K. Chesterton said: 'For anything to be real it must be local.' John has stayed with this locality for very many years. Indeed, it's as though he felt his priesthood needed to be earthed and rooted here. To use a theological phrase: it needed to be 'incarnated' here.

All Saints' parish included one of the most deprived areas of the country, as well as a lot of 'comfortable Britain', situated primarily round the edges of the Park. But even the Park had a more complicated population than might have appeared. I myself knew an old lady in Overstrand Mansions, overlooking the Park, who had seven Nigerian lodgers – though she herself was the widow of a Cabinet Minister in Lloyd George's Government.

John has stayed with Battersea. And the conjunction of Time – the mystery of Time – and the mystery of this place – Battersea – has formed and framed a significant part of John's priesthood. It has led him, for instance, to be a Trustee of the Battersea Churches Housing Trust for many years.

And it also meant that he was able to ensure that all the All Saints' Church site, after the tragic fire, was redeveloped with the Wandsworth Borough Council – under John's gentle but powerful hand – to produce a dual-purpose church that could be used as a day nursery, plus a vicarage, and with 52 dwellings, managed by a co-operative.

'For anything to be real it must be local'. And John's priesthood has been real and local: local and real.

Then there's my second text: 'You shall love the Lord your God with all your heart and with all your soul, and with all your strength, and with all your mind; and your neighbour as yourself.' Without doubt John has felt a special call to love God with his mind – not least since his retirement. He has spent much time researching a treatise on the modern state of matrimony, which has been a marvellous thing to do with all the different aspects of his experience as a priest.

God knows! the state of matrimony (but not just the state of matrimony!) is in chaos at the moment, and needs careful and devoted thought based on experience – marriage as a public and social issue.

In John's thinking and teaching of sociology at Roehampton, he has exercised his mind and heart and priesthood. But it hasn't simply been 'theory'. How could anyone married to Ann, who started as a nurse, and trained as a teacher – teaching in South London – at the Elephant – how could such a one just be a theorist? And how could a parent with three daughters – all of whom have become teachers! And how could anyone with ten grandchildren, think only theoretically about the state of marriage today?

I say again that John wanted to underline how much the word 'regard' has come to mean to him, as he has come to regard the people he has visited and met; as he has talked over with them baptism and marriage and housing and bereavement and just what their jobs in the world have involved.

As he said this, I found myself wanting to say how much people in Battersea have come to regard *him* as a quiet and gentle man of God, as a man of great integrity, wise and humble, and a true 'steward of the mysteries of God'.

The mystery of time is, of course, underlined by anniversaries like John's fiftieth anniversary of priesthood, and draws us inexorably nearer to that horizon beyond which lie even greater 'mysteries of God'.

When I was staying those few days at St Mary's Abbey, West Malling, I picked up one of those hand-written cards, written in elegant script, that you tend to find on Abbey book-stalls and in their tract cases. The particular card had only eight words on it, surrounded by an ocean of margin: 'Life is awareness of the mystery of God'.

John has helped many towards that awareness – to be aware of the mystery at the heart of life – not only in another world than this but here and now, in the Battersea he has loved and served so faithfully.

'Life is the awareness of the mystery of God.'